Learning through Discovery for Young Children

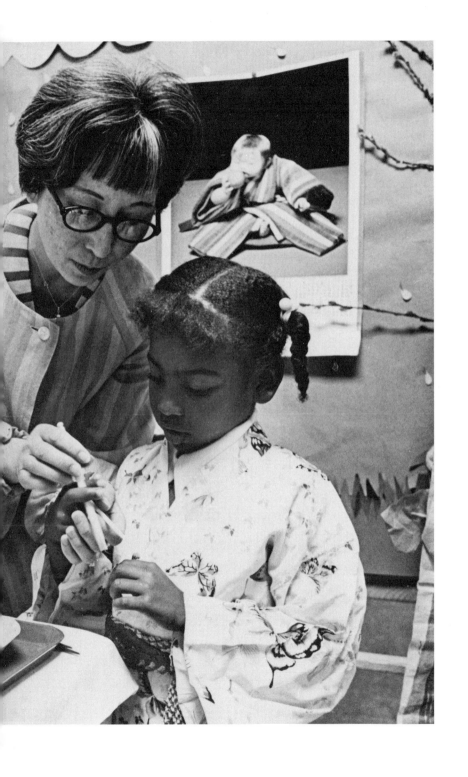

Learning through Discovery for Young Children

SAMUEL G. SAVA

*Executive Director, Institute for
Development of Educational Activities, Inc.
and Vice President for Educational Activities,
Charles F. Kettering Foundation*

McGRAW-HILL BOOK COMPANY

New York   St. Louis   San Francisco

Düsseldorf   London   Mexico   Sydney   Toronto

Library of Congress Cataloging in Publication Data

Sava, Samuel George, date
    Learning through discovery for young children.

    Bibliography: p.
      1.   Learning by discovery.   2.   Education, Preschool.
I.   Title.
LB 1067.S28   372.21   75-5845
ISBN 0-07-054963-X

 234567890 BPBP 798765

The editors for this book were Thomas Quinn and Cheryl Love, the designer was Elaine Gongora, and the production supervisor was Milton Heiberg. It was set in Times Roman by Latham Computertype.

Printed and bound by the Book Press.

2/25/77 RM.   7.95

CONTENTS

Preface

This book stems, in a paradoxical way, from the fact that there already are hundreds of publications, ranging from books to pamphlets, offering teachers and parents advice on educational activities for the preschool child. One might logically wonder whether another publication in the field can provide anything new, or whether it will not simply confuse practitioners even further by adding one more title to a distressingly long bibliography.

Rather than competing with the many other worthwhile items of information about preschool education, however, this publication attempts to make the others more valuable by supplying practitioners with the most essential component of any intelligent preschool program: a rationale or an educational perspective. Lest that sound unduly pretentious or unduly simplistic, let me explain that while I was researching other publications, I was struck both by the number of suggestions available and by the lack of an appropriate explanation of the educational purpose behind the suggestions. I found list upon list of things to do, objects to make, songs to sing, and games to play—but only limited rationale that would help a teacher understand why a child should engage in any of these activities or what result might be expected if he did. Any educational activity should have a purpose; often, however, I found none expressed and was left with the impression that any sort of puttering around would qualify as "developmental."

But even more disturbing than the total lack of rationale in some works was an overly academic rationale in others, which seemed to regard early childhood development exclusively as preparation for formal school work. Typical of this rationale was a stress on preschooling as a guarantee of early reading, IQ gains, high grades for the three-year-old five years hence, and admission to an Ivy League college fifteen years hence.

There is no question that the preschool years are important to maturation of all sorts—cognitive, physical, social, emotional—and that they are the years during which the young human learns with the greatest ease and the greatest pleasure; indeed, as the following pages point out, learning *is* pleasure for children. But it is also certain that these early developmental years can be misused by well-meaning adults who lack a balanced perspective for organizing a preschool environment.

My goal in this book is to offer the practitioner such a perspective. It stresses, on the one hand, that activities should be clearly linked to a developmental purpose, to precise ideas about the *goals* of early childhood education, but it insists, on the other, that there are developmental goals equally as important to a child at this stage of life as preparation for school.

Part I briefly reviews the evolution of early childhood education, cites a few of the major research findings that indicate the importance of properly designed developmental programs for the young child, and proposes a perspective that balances the just claims of cognitive with other kinds of development. Part II builds on the theoretical base proposed in Part I, providing a framework within which a teacher can build an early childhood program that makes educational sense and will stimulate the development of the whole child. Part III discusses specific procedures by which the teacher can create a stimulating learning environment for young children.

The suggestions in Parts I through III have intentionally been limited to a sampling; their purpose is not to prescribe a complete curriculum but to show how a "learning-through-discovery" perspective can be translated into daily preschool practice. At some points the text refers to the bibliography as a source for more ideas, but it does not attempt to compete with the rich and varied collection available elsewhere. Rather, this publication invites the teacher to use his or her own creativity in designing an educational environment; it invites him or her to function as an active shaper of the learning process rather than as the passive servant of an overly prescriptive, minutely detailed set of commandments.

Acknowledgments

Early childhood education continues to receive attention throughout the United States for a variety of reasons. Significant among these would be the fact that more and more parents are now realizing the importance of the early years. Of equal importance is the fact that more and more women have entered the labor force and are seeking appropriate care for their children.

Whatever the reasons, and there are others, the Institute for Development of Educational Activities, Inc. (|I|D|E|A|), an affiliate of the Charles F. Kettering Foundation, has been deeply interested in the issue of early development of youngsters and the impact that experiences (or lack of) have on individual children. A major study was therefore undertaken a few years ago on the status of early schooling in the United States. The results of this survey were recently published by McGraw-Hill in a series identified as "|I|D|E|A| Reports on Schooling." During the years of the study, I had the opportunity to review many of the publications, curriculum guides, and other documents relating to early childhood education, and I was surprised by the number that recommended activities for young children without identifying the "whys" of such activities. This book is not one in the series although it was stimulated, as noted, by the review of the materials collected. It offers, I believe, an appropriate perspective for the needs of early childhood education.

Dr. David Buzzard of the Charles F. Kettering Foundation edited the final version of the book, and I thank him for his valuable assistance.

ABOUT THE PHOTOGRAPHS

My special thanks to Mike Naas of the Early Childhood Education Project, Dayton (Ohio) City Schools and to Dan Patterson for their many hours spent photographing the early childhood education scenes shown in *Learning through Discovery for Young Children*. And to Eric Hendrickson of the Charles F. Kettering Foundation for bringing those photographs together as part of the text.

Learning through Discovery for Young Children

PART I

Why
Early Childhood
Education?

The first experiments with early childhood education were initiated to care for children who had been abandoned, by choice or necessity, by their parents—and the entire concept has threatened to become an educational orphan ever since. In France, in the late 1700's, *crèches d'asile* and *salles d'asile* were established to protect unsupervised youngsters from the harmful influences of the streets. In 1816, a Scottish mill owner named Robert Owen opened a "preparatory school" for infants from one to six years old, out of a concern for the children of his employees, but the school was not intended to teach them anything—merely to relieve the drabness of their surroundings and the joylessness of their lives with games and organized play. Around the turn of the nineteenth century, a group of tenement owners in Rome, upset about the damage that children were doing to property while their mothers worked, looked around for someone to keep these prospective delinquents occupied during the day—and came up with Maria Montessori, Italy's first woman physician. Dr. Montessori did, indeed, occupy the children's hands and minds in more worthwhile pursuits. In fact, she taught a number of her Roman "disadvantaged" to read and write. Her methods are still regarded by many developmental psychologists as the most successful attempt to match a child's growing intellectual potential with opportunities for turning those possibilities into realitites. Nevertheless, this educational outcome was regarded as little more than a fringe benefit by the landlords who had financed Dr. Montessori's remarkable experiments.

To a great degree, this custodial view of early childhood education has persisted into the eighth decade of the twentieth century. "Real" school, we believe, starts with first grade or, at the earliest, with kindergarten; all anyone can hope to do with children before then, according to this view, is to keep them happy puttering around with blocks and stuffed animals while Mom works or goes shopping, and feed them peanut-butter sandwiches and cocoa when they get restless.

In fact, early childhood programs have been supported for almost every reason *except* "education." The federal government opened day-care centers during the Depression and again during World War II—but to provide jobs for unemployed teachers in the first case, and to free women for work in defense plants in the second case. Only in the late 1960's, with the introduction of Operation Head Start by the federal government, was early childhood education recognized in a public way as a genuinely educational service rather than as a glorified form of baby-sitting or a kind of preventive detention. And even Head Start, because of its emphasis on the problems of "economically deprived" children, left the impression that the major function of early childhood education is to serve as a substitute for the home.

RESEARCHERS AGREE THAT EARLY DEVELOPMENT IS CRUCIAL

Early childhood education is not a substitute for the home, nor can it begin to provide the warmth, intimacy, and sense of security which every child has a right to expect from his parents. Intelligently viewed, early childhood education— conveniently referred to as ECE hereafter—is an attempt to stimulate the development of the human mind *at the time when it develops most rapidly and with the greatest ease.*

All over the United States today, educators, politicians, citizens' groups, and other guardians of the public welfare are arguing for an increase in the amount of money and other resources we devote to educational research. Progressive industries,

A major part of a child's intellectual development takes place during the early years.

they point out, allocate about 10 percent of their funds to research, while education sets aside only about 1 percent.

One might have more faith in these analogies if education had demonstrated more ability to act on the research it already has. However, the facts about child development—and the clear implications for ECE—have been before educators and public policymakers for almost fifty years. This is not to say that additional research is not needed. On the contrary, we need vast amounts of additional knowledge about these beginning years. But we must also put to use the information we have now.

Let us begin with a few quotes, dating from Arnold Gesell in 1925:

The brain grows at a tremendous rate during the preschool age, reaching almost its mature bulk before the age of six . . . . Never again will his mind, his character, his spirit advance as rapidly as in this formative preschool period of growth. Never again will we have an equal chance to lay the foundation of mental health (p. 11).

Research studies by Benjamin Bloom and his associates at the University of Chicago indicate that, in terms of intelligence measured at age seventeen, about 50 percent of the development takes place between conception and age four; 30 percent occurs between ages four and eight; and about 20 percent takes place between ages eight and seventeen. In other words, as much of the development takes place in the first four years of life as in the next thirteen.

More recently (1973), Burton L. White of Harvard University's Graduate School of Education concluded:

If a three-year-old is six months or more behind in academically relevant areas, such as language and problem-solving skills, he is not likely to ever be successful in his future educational career. There are exceptions to this generalization, but the results of Head Start, Follow Through and other remedial programs clearly support this statement for large numbers of American children (p.6).

Such statements sound so flat and final that they produce almost a "scare" effect. Moreover, such statements, based on the research of highly qualified investigators, do not seem at all to buttress the case for preschool, since most programs in this country do not begin until after three. If "it's all over" by the age of three, why bother?

First, I maintain that it is *not* all over by the age of three—neither in the cognitive areas nor in other realms of development. There has been considerable dispute about Bloom's percentage figures for the developmental rate of intelligence and about White's interpretation of the data. Edward Zigler, former director of the U.S. Office of Child Development and director of the child development program at Yale University, argues that cognitive development is a continuous process, and asks, "We do not know when all cognitive development is over, so how could we know when half of it is over?" (1973, p. 18). While apparently accepting Dr. Bloom's findings, John Fischer, former president of Teachers College at Columbia University, added an important qualifying note in a January 1968 report to President Lyndon Johnson for the National Advisory Council on the Education of Disadvantaged Children:

This is no ground for believing that a child's academic fate is sealed by his seventh birthday, but it means that a community that seriously wants to improve its children's opportunities will start them to school early.

Jerome Kagan, the noted developmental psychologist, recently conducted a cross-cultural study of the cognitive development of Guatemalan children; he reported that in an isolated Indian village the three-year-old counterparts of active 11-year-old Guatemalan children were silent, inactive, and somewhat isolated with their mothers. Most of these children remain passive and apathetic until five or six years of age. However, when groups of children from the same Guatemalan village were assessed at later ages ranging from five to twelve years for perceptual inference, memory recall, and recognition, differences between rural Guatemalan children and urban Guatemalan and American children were found to be sharply diminished and, in some cases, to disappear. Kagan concluded that cognitive development during the early years is more flexible; the main influence seems to be the time of emergence rather than the ultimate level of development.

Also, note that the research cited here focuses on specifically cognitive development, principally as measured by IQ tests. These tests themselves have come under sharp attack in recent years on the grounds of inadequacy and inaccuracy. Assuming that, for most purposes, IQ tests do measure growth in some facets of intelligence, particularly those that lead to success in school, it is also true that academic intelligence is only one aspect of human development, and not necessarily the most important. Many outstanding humans have succeeded despite difficulties in school: Thomas Edison was dismissed from first grade as "unteachable," Winston Churchill was last in his class in preparatory school, Edgar Allen Poe and James Whistler were expelled from West Point, Charles Darwin dropped out of both medical school and divinity school before taking up (to his father's profound disappointment) a career as a naturalist, and Albert Einstein was an indifferent student in grammar school. It was his uncle, showing him tricks with numbers in the evening, who stimulated Einstein's interest in mathematics. In many fields of human endeavor, school grades have virtually no relationship to success in life; we make a serious mistake if we assume that preschooling succeeds only if it produces straight-A students or gains in measured IQ.

In addition, many of the statements made about the "failures" of preschooling stem from widely publicized experiments such as Head Start and Follow Through. Though some care was taken to include a minority of middle-class children where this was possible, the great majority of children attending these programs were from disadvantaged homes—not *bad* homes, but homes typically lacking the environmental richness, variety, and interest that middle-class parents provide as a matter of course, and which developmental specialists refer to as "the hidden curriculum." If we are to rescue such children from a life of scholastic difficulty, it would seem, from the limited research cited, that we will probably have to begin much earlier than the age of three and finance highly expensive programs that focus on the home and parents as well as to follow through with quality preschool programs. But the failure of our past inadequate remedial measures with environmentally handicapped children should not be allowed to discredit the value of well-designed preschool programs for children who have already gotten a solid start in life from their homes.

For these children (and they compose the majority of youngsters) as well as the others, it is *not* "all over by age three." There is plenty of growing room left for them along all sorts of dimensions—aesthetically, socially, morally, physically, and emotionally as well as "cognitively," narrowly defined. All are genuine forms of learning, even though the schools and colleges do not stress them, and each can be as important to a human life as those strictly scholastic achievements that are measured by grades. Developing an aesthetic sense—for example, what is beautiful?—and beginning to learn how to express that sense in line, color, space, and form may sound unimportant and even frivolous to a parent who thinks of "learning" only in terms of mathematics and English grammar. Apart from bringing deep pleasure to many adult lives, however, a well-developed aesthetic sense is the crucial element in the professional lives of artists, architects, photographers, and the designers of everything from book jackets to cities.

Bringing together the research that has been cited above and the foregoing comments, I would advance this perspective on early childhood development programs as the rationale for what follows in this volume:

1. No matter what the percentages of cognitive development that occur at certain ages, development takes place most rapidly from birth to age seven.

2. These are also the years during which the human seems to learn most quickly, most easily, and most pleasurably.

3. Much learning during these years happens naturally, without the planned, conscious intervention of parents or teachers.

4. But much more learning could occur if we made intelligent use of these early years through instruction properly attuned to the young child's interests and capacities.

5. Some of the learning possible through a well-planned ECE program is helpful to children during later school years.

6. Other forms of learning, while not measured or rewarded by the schools, are inherently worthwhile and enhance a youngster's chances for a free and happy adult life.

7. A good preschool program, therefore, while not guaranteeing high grades or advances in IQ, is an advantage to a child—but only if we know how to use these years during which a youngster learns most easily.

How does a teacher begin bridging the gap between research and practice?

PLANNED STIMULATION FOR DEVELOPMENT

During the 1930s and 1940s, many specialists in child rearing believed that intelligence was fixed at birth by a child's inheritance from his parents. Consequently, there was no point in "pushing" a child to learn anything; he would learn naturally, and the best course of action any parents could take—apart from providing love and a warm home—was to leave the child alone.

Since then, however, a great deal of evidence has indicated that intelligence is *not* fixed at birth and that a youngster's mental development is influenced, for better or worse, by his environment and experience. From his earliest years, especially those before the normal school-starting age, he can be stimulated by the right kinds of experience so that at maturity he will be genuinely more intelligent than he would have been without that stimulation. "There is no evidence that guided stimulation has ever harmed young children," comments Maya Pines in her book entitled *Revolution in Learning* (1967, p. 49), "but there is plenty of evidence that no human being of high ability has ever grown up without it."

I purposely use the word *stimulation* above instead of *education* because, though the terms can be taken to mean the same thing, adults commonly misinterpret education when it is used within the context of early childhood. They conceive of education as they have known it—as formal instruction in specific subjects for specific purposes in which achievement can be rather precisely measured. Unfortunately along with this, for many parents, is a memory of a series of unhappy events and environments associated with formal schooling.

Perhaps the best way to explain stimulation is to mention a series of fascinating experiments conducted with infants in institutions such as orphanages and foundling homes. For years, developmental researchers have been appalled at, and intrigued by, the slow rate of development of apparently normal children in such institutions. Pines, in the following excerpt from the book, describes what they found:

Though babies normally learn to sit without support at age of ten months, infants in an orphanage in Teheran became so apathetic and retarded that fewer than half of them learned to sit up alone by the age of two years....At the age of four, 85 per cent of them still failed to walk alone (1967,p.172).

This degree of retardation is extreme, but it has its analogies in United States institutions. Apparently normal infants with average or even above-average IQ's were much slower to reach, to grasp, to turn their heads, to raise their heads or try turning over—all important stages in a newborn's development. The explanation first advanced was that these children had been deprived of their mothers and that the lack of love and individual attention resulted in retardation. Later, however, some psychologists began wondering whether a more basic problem might be the lack of sights, sounds, and events that might stimulate these children to respond. As Pines put it:

Babies in such institutions spent their whole time waiting for something interesting to happen to them—and eventually gave up. To protect them from drafts and from getting their heads stuck between bars, their cribs were lined with white covers, which acted like blinders; they could see nothing on either side of them. The ceilings were also white, without anything interesting to look at. Nobody talked to them, and they heard precious little speech of any kind. They had no toys. They took their nourishment alone, from bottles that were propped up for them (1967, p. 173).

One by one, in various places, psychologists began experimenting with institutionalized infants. The prevailing blandness of their white surroundings was "enriched" with brightly colored sheets and dangling mobiles, and the crib covers—a necessary safety precaution—were varied with animal and flower designs. Infants were placed on their stomachs for short periods several times a day, and the solid white headboards on their cribs were replaced with clear plastic, allowing them to see activity in the room.

The results were fast and dramatic. Infants who had lain motionless for most of the day began raising their heads and following the passage of a doctor or nurse through the room. They stared at the mobiles, then began swinging their fists at them and, finally, reaching out and grasping for them. Formerly silent, apathetic babies smiled, began to coo and even chuckle at the bright new objects in their previously drab, changeless world.

Just as the human body needs nutrition for growth, the human mind needs stimulation. The human digestive system cannot work unless it has something to work *on:* food. Similarly, the digestive system of the mind has an appetite for its own sort of food to work on: stimulation. Just as human muscles need exercise for development—the opportunity to run, grasp, lift, stretch, pull, push—so the human mind needs the exercise provided by difference and novelty, by the interesting, amusing, and puzzling. If the infants mentioned above could talk, they might be saying: There's something new. What is it? What does it do? What if I hit it? Hey, it swings back and forth! Now it's stopped. It was more fun to watch when it was swinging. I'll hit it again.

And so development accelerates, picks up speed, and continues as long as some different stimulus, proportioned to a human's age, appears and in some way challenges or intrigues the mind. A seventy-year-old human can still grow in interesting ways as long as he happens upon or seeks out some stimulation that triggers the old, wonderful questions: There's a new thing. What does it do? What if I hit it?

A good preschool program provides stimulation proportioned to the age and developmental stage of the children it serves. Stimulation thus does not mean the same thing as education, though it is an essential part of education. Stimulation connotes exposure to a wide range of experiences—sights and sounds, activities, chances to do things—which, while planned, need not be undertaken in any special order or, for that matter, completed in their entirety. Not everyone has to learn the same things at the same time. Perhaps the basic distinction between good early childhood instruction and traditional formal instruction such as one encounters in the first grade and beyond is this: In the typical school, the teacher leads the student step by step through a planned curriculum that has a definite sequence—the same curriculum for every child—and equips children with the knowledge and skills that educational experts believe they must possess. In ECE, the teacher *helps the student develop his own curriculum* by working with him in an environment that is rich in possibilities for many kinds of learning. To state it another way, the elementary school teacher tries to interest children in things which the school board believes they should learn; the ECE teacher tries to help children learn from things in which they display a natural interest.

There are excellent reasons for this freedom—again, drawn from research into child development. They bear essentially on what psychologist J. McVicker Hunt (1961) has called "the problem of the match," and which I will say more about in a moment.

Human capacities, both mental and physical, seem to develop according to a definite sequence in every child. For example, the infant invariably learns to grasp objects before he or she learns to roll over. One infant may learn to grasp earlier than another of the same age, but in both, the basic human abilities seem to unfold in the same order.

Each of these activities requires what is known as a *schema*, a convergence or fitting-together of mental and physical capacities

The development of a child's mental and physical abilities can be stimulated and enhanced during the preschool years.

of certain kinds. Learning to grasp, for example, requires the infant to be able to curl his fingers around an object when his brain, transmitting information from his sense of touch, tells him that he has encountered the object. At first, he doesn't even use his eyes for this; later on, however, he will coordinate sight and touch along with the mental act of *wanting* to grasp.

Similarly, walking and talking require other schemata. As these activities become more complex, the appropriate schema more and more involves the mind: the interpretation of information that the sensory organs transmit to the brain, the ability to shift that information around in different patterns so that the child develops ideas, and conscious decisions to act in one way rather than another.

This development can be *stimulated*—and enhanced—through a variety of experiences that encourage development. However, it cannot be *forced*—made to happen before the child's mental and physical capacities are inclined to learning of a certain kind.

And therein lies the problem of the match—matching a child's readiness to learn something new with the opportunity for learning. If the distance between what a child already knows and what he is encouraged to learn is not too great for his intellectual muscles to carry him—what psychologists call "the proper discrepancy"—he will not only learn but *will take pleasure in doing so.* If that distance, on the other hand, is too great for the youngster's intellectual readiness and/or physical readiness, he or she may show fear or distress; if placed under continuing pressure, the distance could be damaging. And if, finally, there is little or no discrepancy—no opportunity for the child to advance beyond what he or she already knows or can do—the child is likely to become bored. The challenge for any good ECE program, then, is one of solving this problem of the match.

But how do we know when a child's mental and physical capacities have developed to a point that disposes him to learn something new—particularly when rates of development vary with individual children?

The answer, quite simply, is that we *don't* know—and that is why no good ECE program can impose a single "curriculum" on all its young enrollees. Instead, ECE must offer children a variety of guided opportunities for learning and allow each youngster to *act as the agent of his own development.*

Such a notion runs contrary to everything that most adults believe about education and school. For most of us, learning is or has been a chore, a job, a duty that required considerable self-discipline and an outside force (a teacher, a test, pressure from parents for good grades, from an employer for improved performance) to supplement that self-discipline with institutional discipline. For a number of adults, learning is no fun.

But for children, amazingly, learning *is* fun. Every parent has heard his or her own infant "talk" at great length before the child could pronounce a single word, baffle-gabbling on in some private, secret monologue of childhood, producing absolutely no sense but what is, apparently, highly satisfying noise. And every parent has seen his or her preschool child "read"—sitting soberly on a couch, speaking aloud some scrambled story line, turning at appropriate intervals the pages of a book which, as often as not, is held upside down. Parents remember such episodes in the development of their children, but they do not often recognize their significance: Given a chance, *children actively pursue learning and clearly take pleasure in it.* In Robert White's observations, children have a drive for competence, an unconscious but nonetheless powerful yearning to discover who they are by discovering what they can do.

The built-in motivation to learn, while genuine, must nevertheless be qualified. Children want to learn—but not just anything. They want to learn things that they are *ready* to learn, and the surest test of that readiness is their interest (or lack of it) in whatever is offered as an opportunity for learning.

That is where the ECE teacher comes in. The previous remarks may leave the false impression that preschool education is mainly a matter of getting out of the way and allowing the children to do what comes naturally.

It is not. While teachers should refrain from trying to push children to do or investigate or learn about the things that they believe children *should* be interested in, they must nonetheless take a highly active, professional role in helping children help themselves. They must be able to recognize and learn to interpret the symptoms of boredom or of unhappiness in a youngster: Does unhappiness mean that a child has exhausted one kind of learning experience and wants to move on to something new—or does it mean that the child is baffled by what he or she is doing, and should either return to something simpler or be given some adult help? In many cases the child's unhappiness might not be related to educational environment but rather to the home. What can be done in such cases? Perhaps something, perhaps nothing; the teacher may be the only adult in a position to diagnose the problem and attempt to solve or modify it. Is the child physically able to handle the tasks selected or provided? For example, is the child being forced to utilize his or her eyes

Following pages: **A child at rest may simply be that—resting. Or maybe the child is frustrated by the difficulty of a task or bored by its simplicity.**

in such ways that could place them under undue strain? Is a youngster better off alone in certain situations, or does he or she prefer to be with two or three other children? Older children, adolescents, and college students may be able to explain to a sympathetic teacher why they find a program of instruction at fault; preschool children, however, find it much more difficult, for they have not reached the state of self-consciousness and self-understanding at which they can express such puzzling emotions and ideas.

Hence the teacher or team of teachers of preschool children must, in a sense, speak for children who cannot speak for themselves. They must try to solve the problem of the match. There is no magic formula for this. They must learn by experience, exchange knowledge about individual children, be familiar, to the extent possible, with the latest research on child development, and decide on the basis of intuition, experience, and association with the home when to step in and when to stay out.

This book tries to offer some hints along the way, but it is not a teaching manual. It is, rather, a guide to help the preschool teacher and the preschool director to develop or perhaps define their own program for early childhood education. Chapters in this book suggest specific stimulation or activity centers and try to make clear the relation between centers and the suggested materials and activities.

Many of the activities may seem aimless. The teacher should remember, in going through this book, the distinction made earlier between education and stimulation, and the tendency of adults to feel that if a child is not learning something clearly recognizable as "school work"—reading, writing, figuring—the activity is simply child's play.

The important educational facts are that children learn *through* play and that they do not distinguish work *from* play; to children, interesting work *is* play. The important developmental fact is that stimulating children's minds through activities not normally and regularly offered in the home strengthens their cognitive ability to tackle the increasingly difficult learning tasks they will face in the decades ahead.

Lest this sound somewhat fuzzy or Utopian, consider these conclusions from J. McVicker Hunt, a preeminent student of child development who, after analyzing the evidence of dozens of other scholars, had this to say:

> It appears that the counsel from experts on child-rearing during the third and much of the fourth decades of the twentieth century to let children be while they grow, and to avoid excessive stimulation, was highly unfortunate. . . . It is no longer unreasonable to consider that it may be feasible to discover ways to govern the encounters that children have with their environments, especially during the early years of their development, to achieve a substantially faster rate of intellectual development and a substantially higher adult level of intellectual capacity (1961, p. 362).

Dr. Hunt emphasizes intellectual capacity here. While there has been research experimentation to justify this optimism, there have also been enough program failures to make us wonder whether we can ever translate the research into practice for large numbers of children in a practical, socially affordable way.

No matter. Intellectual development is only one form of human development, and much remains to be discovered about the possibilities of helping children discover and realize more of their potential through planned stimulation. Though our society's system of rewarding its educators has yet to reflect the fact, the possibilities for the teacher of preschool children are, in the most profoundly professional sense, both more exciting and important than those for the university teacher of graduate students. If this guide helps a few more preschool teachers convert more of their young charges' possibilities into actualities—helps them, in Dr. Hunt's words, "discover ways to govern the encounters that children have with their environments"—it will have served its purpose.

PART II

Putting the Program Together

Though there is no one way of putting a preschool program together, most good programs have much in common. Perhaps the basic similarity is that *all center around the child.* Since this may sound like nothing more than a useless truism, it is worth pointing out that most school programs center around the curriculum and its standards: the thrust is to encourage the student to come up to the school's standards, to absorb the information, and to develop the skills reflected in a relatively inflexible curriculum.

By contrast, the child-centered nature of the preschool is an orderly attempt to enable the child to explore as many of his own interests and abilities as possible, in an atmosphere that offers both *support* and *stimulation.* The curriculum of the preschool is an intelligent assembly of *opportunities* for learning, not a compulsory schedule for learning to which every child must adhere.

The twin characteristics of support and stimulation bear on what was said in Part I about the proper discrepancy between what a child knows and his readiness to learn something new. One of the simplest ways to explain the interdependence of support and stimulation in the preschool environment is to quote the Swiss psychologist Jean Piaget's maxim, "The half-familiar teaches." The child does not readily learn anything that is totally new and strange to him; rather, he builds on what he already

19

knows, stepping forward from it as from one rock to another to cross a stream.

The characteristic drive of the preschool child is toward greater autonomy and independence. Where earlier, at home, he developed a sense of trust in his parents and the other members of his family, he now needs to develop a distinctive pride in himself, to strengthen his confidence in his own ability to do things. That confidence must be built up slowly, by giving every youngster an early experience of success in small learning steps so that he develops an eagerness to take larger steps without undue fear of failure. Thus the preschool environment, while stimulating him to try new and different things, must not represent too great a departure from the environment with which the child is already familiar. That environment, in turn, is a composite of (1) the teacher or teachers, (2) the curriculum, (3) the physical environment, (4) the social environment, and (5) the tie between home environment and the school environment.

THE TEACHER

The role of the teacher (or team of teachers) in a preschool is both more difficult and more interesting than that of the teacher in a traditional school. It is more difficult because the preschool teacher cannot rely heavily on a structured curriculum and rigid classroom organization and scheduling to carry her through the day. It is more interesting because the preschool teacher has more latitude in devising activities that will meet the changing interests and developing abilities of her young charges. Her function, essentially, is twofold: (1) to organize a preschool environment that offers every child a variety of opportunities for self-exploration and learning and (2) to observe each child in order to interpret his or her individual, distinctive needs and "moments of readiness," adapting the total environment—selecting the right pieces of it—to capitalize on those moments when a child is ready to advance. Perhaps no aspect of the preschool learning environment is more important than the teacher's willingness—a blend of professionalism and humility—to learn *from* each child in order to help him learn.

This requires, at a minimum, a teacher with the professional background to recognize and understand the special characteristics of his or her young clientele, and the implications of those characteristics for instruction. Among those characteristics as identified by James L. Hymes, Jr., in his book entitled *Teaching the Child Under Six* (1974) and paraphrased here are these:

● *Young children are not good sitters.* Some day—five or ten years from now—they will be able to sit, relax, loaf, stretch out, and stay put. Right now, they are on the go, bursting with energy, and they need space. "Chairs ought to be the least used equipment in early childhood education" (p. 37).

● *Young children are not good at keeping quiet.* Though a continuing racket will get them down, noise to children of this age is natural, a companion of happy activity and not at all an obstacle to learning. Consequently, the space in which they work must be designed so that the noise made by some does not disrupt the concentration of the others.

● *Young children are shy.* They come from homes in which, for the past two years or so, they have been the center of attention as probably the youngest. Consequently, while they are both ready and eager to meet with others, they can be easily overwhelmed and frightened by large groups. The preschool environment must introduce them to groups gradually and must afford each a chance to draw back by himself into solitary activity from time to time.

● *Young children are highly egocentric.* In a few years, youngsters of this age will be able to think of themselves as members of a social group, as part of a class or family. Right now, they are overwhelmed by their sense of individuality: their vocabulary is characterized by extensive (to an adult, excessive) use of *I, my,* and *me.* The preschool must allow for this extreme sense of individuality rather than pressuring children into an early socialization. It must make room for the child's desire to be recognized and admired as a unique human being, quite apart from his membership in a class of other youngsters who exhibit many of the same traits.

● *Young children want to feel proud, big, and important.* For all their desire to be recognized as unique, youngsters of this age really cannot do much of anything well. They are sur-

rounded by reminders—in the form of adults, older brothers and sisters, by height, weight, and size—of things they *cannot* do. Hence they are much more susceptible than adults to failure; the preschool environment must offer every child an opportunity to succeed at *something,* no matter how small or seemingly trivial to an adult—and the teacher must match every child's faltering abilities with tasks that each can achieve.

• *Young children have a dream world.* Until they can build up a record of success in school, in games, in life, children need a world in which they can make their own rules, where everything comes out right. Life brings everyone a share of defeat, and it will bring children their share to enable them to scale their hopes down to a practical measure of possibility; no educational program has to trim youngsters of this age down to their own size—they are already painfully aware of that size. On the contrary, every preschool program should make room for a fantasy life in which every child can see himself as the hero.

• *Young children are very tender.* For all their bragging about their modest accomplishments, preschool children are intensely dependent on adults and others for proof that they are loved and respected. They need a warm, safe environment. The teacher of older children may properly worry about keeping some distance between herself and her students; the teacher of preschool children need not. More important than words of praise are signs of genuine affection—a touch, a squeeze, even a kiss. Consequently, the preschool teacher should be a person who has a spontaneous, unforced liking for children as well as the emotional maturity to distinguish between a child's need for affection and his tendency to take advantage of anyone who displays it.

• *Young children are beginners.* Despite the most careful instructions and the most elaborate explanations, they have a capacity for doing everything wrong. Judged by adult standards of human performance—particularly if those standards are not modified by a parent's love—they fail constantly. If a teacher cannot muster affection for every one of her students (and this

The preschool teacher who thoughtfully allows room in the program for a child's fantasy world is really providing a zone of security where the child can literally be king or queen.

is difficult for every parent to maintain all the time), she must cultivate *patience.* The teacher is in mid-life, but the children are just beginning theirs, and they have lots of time.

● *Young children are hungry for stimulation.* Never again will any teacher have students more eager to learn, more curious, than in preschool. Boredom is rarely their problem; keeping up with them, matching their energies, satisfying their curiosity usually is. The preschool classroom should not be a place to slow them down, to satisfy the teacher's adult craving for some sense of order; rather, it should cater to the child's constantly self-renewing wonder about this amazing world which is so new to him. The teacher must think of the classroom—of the entire preschool environment, indoors and out—as her ally, and must arrange it so that it carries some of the teaching task because it is so varied and interesting a place.

● *Young children are earthy, practical, concrete-minded.* Though some of them demonstrate an amazing facility with words, an impressive "gift of gab," they learn best through things: concrete objects they can pick up, turn, drop, arrange, stare at. At their stage of human development, they are still trying to bridge the gap between the actual and the symbolic, between the spoken or written word for *paint* and the colorful, delightfully messy thing itself. The preschool must not be in any hurry to impress upon children the importance and use of words; for them understanding comes through the manipulation of the real thing.

● *Young children are acquiescent.* Adult favor means a great deal to them, so they are more willing than older children or other adults to go along with whatever the teacher seems to want. Every child has his moments of rebellion, of course, and some children exhibit constant behavior problems. Given a teacher whom they like, though, and a task not too difficult for them to carry out, they will do what the teacher wishes even if the task does not interest them. This means that a good preschool teacher must be careful not to impose her own preferences on children, or obtain their apparent approval with the gentle bullying of a smile. The job, to repeat, is not to run children through a preconceived curriculum, but to devise activities based on their built-in interest in learning.

• *Young children are illiterate*. Though a few children begin to read as early as the age of three, the great majority of those through five years of age cannot—nor should anyone be anxious about this. No preschool should promise to teach children to read, nor, on the other hand, should it make a point of promising *not* to teach children to read. It should offer some stimuli for the child who is approaching the "moment of readiness" for reading, and a teacher alert to such an interest. Like any other new skill, however, reading is one that children are generally interested in developing. With all the other stimuli toward it around them—the example of parents and other family members in their homes and the constant use of printed words in advertising, for instance—they will need little urging when the proper developmental moment arrives.

Finally, despite these notes about what young children are as a group, the preschool teacher must remember above all that they are *not* a group. Most exhibit the characteristics outlined above, but each is primarily an individual. It may be difficult to find any sign of shyness in one child, any indication of tenderness in another, or any evidence of acquiescence in a third. While these traits may help a teacher understand the special humans she is dealing with, they provide no psychological x-ray for any individual child.

Provided that the preschool classroom offers each child sufficient freedom of expression, the best index to his or her state of development—mental, physical, emotional—is behavior. The teacher must learn to diagnose this behavior as the symptom or external clue to an internal condition—boredom, curiosity, fear, envy—and respond to it. She should encourage a diversity of methods for solving problems. Children will need to verify results, and such verification should depend as much as possible on the results of their activities.

The teacher should attempt to bring a number of children into each activity. They should be offered encouragement to work together and to actively experience their activities rather than being told about them.

Children will carry out their activities in different ways. These actions will enable the teacher to understand the child and in turn be able to offer suggestions, define new goals, and establish new learning opportunities. Children should not be kept at one activity until they have mastered it. The primary goal should be the experiences acquired in solving a problem. The teacher can add to these experiences by offering conflicting evidence leading toward various and possible solutions.

Especially at the outset, the preschool teacher will have to learn the proper response through a process of observation—a process that requires generous amounts of patience, humility, enthusiasm, and humor as well as a sharp eye for each child's daily, weekly, and monthly progress. Choosing the proper response to a child's behavior is vastly simplified if the teacher has diverse curriculum activities and a rich array of materials to choose from. An example of such activities is presented in the discussion of the activity centers. Finally, the teacher should establish appropriate methods of evaluation by which she or he may judge the quality and success of the ECE program.

CURRICULUM

The "things" of learning, the materials with which a preschool is furnished, can be as varied as the teacher's imagination. In a recent study conducted by the Institute for Development of Educational Activities, Inc., on Early Schooling in the United States, a list of twenty-eight curricular areas and activities was compiled by a group of early childhood specialists as part of the evaluation process to observe the degree of structure in these areas. The list included the following, along with the identification of materials and equipment needed to support the activities (1973, pp. 96–107).

Informal arithmetic	Informal reading readiness
Formal arithmetic	Formal reading readiness
Art	Reading
Foreign languages	Informal science
Informal language	Formal science
Formal language	Informal social studies
Informal music	Formal social studies
Formal music	Blocks
Music instrument instruction	Carpentry

Cooking	Nature walks
Dramatization and role playing	Outdoor play
Organized group games	Rhythms
Informal rest	Story time
Naps	Trips

But curriculum is much more than things, much more than an atmosphere of freedom and trust. Preschool should be a serious learning enterprise, and if it is to be that, all its elements must be chosen in relation to an underlying rationale: What are the paints and sandboxes, the freedom and the songs, intended to achieve? Curriculum, in other words, begins with a statement of learning objectives.

An example might be the objectives listed below, chosen from the *Prekindergarten Teacher's Guide* (1970-71) of the Dayton (Ohio) Public Schools:

TO HELP CHILDREN
1. Develop an understanding of themselves and a wholesome self-concept.
2. Develop a sense of responsibility and self-confidence, and feeling of security and acceptance.
3. Stimulate concern, understanding and acceptance of children and adults.
4. Live freely and happily in a group.
5. Strenghten inner emotional controls and greater self-discipline.
6. Increase independence in meeting and solving problems.
7. Promote health and physical growth.
8. Develop sensorimotor skills, motor coordination and control.
9. Observe, discover, experiment and acquire information.
10. Extend their understanding of and clarify their concepts of the world in which they live.
11. Increase the use of language skills and communication skills.
12. Develop self-expression through experiences in art, music, dance and literature.
13. Experience success and achievement.
14. Develop a favorable attitude toward learning and school.
15. Exhibit wholesome feelings toward themselves and others.

TO HELP PARENTS
1. Develop skills in helping children achieve a feeling of dignity and worth.
2. Understand the specific role they can play in the physical, mental,

social and emotional growth of their children.
3. Improve the quality of parent-child interaction.
4. Increase the interest of parents in their children's school.
5. Strenghten home-school cooperation.

These are general goals; translating them into an ECE program requires the professional teacher's knowledge of the level of skill children normally exhibit during the preschool years, so that the program can be designed to stimulate the further development of those skills.

THE SOCIAL ENVIRONMENT

Social environment is a somewhat stuffy but useful term that covers the children attending a preschool and the formal and informal ways they are grouped for all the activities that go on in the preschool. The traditional school in most cases groups children for study by a single criterion: age. More and more schools, however, are experimenting with "multi-age grouping" because of the evidence that ability levels vary among young children of similar age, for a variety of reasons. Thus one level of instruction would be inappropriate for a number of children from different age levels and different environmental backgrounds.

Under this multi-age concept (sometimes referred to as the "family concept"), children are grouped according to an *age-span*—usually two, sometimes three years, depending on the maturity of younger children. Instead of dividing them along chronological lines as the traditional school does—three's together, four's together, five's together—children are divided into groups that cut across age-lines.

One of the advantages of this arrangement is that children can learn from each other through imitation, just as they do in a family. If properly managed by the teacher, young children form associations and relationships that cut across age-lines and tend to follow more natural lines of interest, energy, ability, and so on.

Older children help younger children learn things that they themselves learned not very long ago. In doing so, the older children themselves learn—by displaying their skills and demonstrating their competence, by explaining things so that someone younger and less experienced can understand, and by assuming responsibility for others less advanced.

For their part, younger children find in their older companions models that are closer to their reach than adults are. Indeed, under the multi-age grouping concept, other children become an important part of the curriculum. Everyone learns from everyone else, in constantly shifting contexts as the activity of each group moves from outdoor play to painting to singing to work in the various areas described in the following chapters. Hence, if it's properly managed by the teacher, learning becomes a cooperative and constructive endeavor.

"If properly managed by the teacher..." is an important qualification. No form of class organization provides a magic formula for overcoming common educational problems such as the emotional harm done to a youngster when he sees his class-mates constantly out performing him—or, for that matter, the emotional harm done to a youngster who constantly excels his classmates, and grows up equating success in life with success at getting high grades. The multi-age concept does, however, enable the teacher to give every child, no matter what the level of his ability, a regular experience of success.

Again, no matter how clever a curriculum, how well-designed the physical facilities in a preschool, it is the teacher or prefera-bly teachers working together with parents who make the environment.

The social environment also includes planning and scheduling. The child enters an unfamiliar environment when he first walks into a preschool, and he needs to get his bearings in time as well as in space. He needs to rely on the recurrence of certain regular and routine activities to help him place the day in a comprehensive context. Part of his sense of security in his home grows out of his knowledge that the day starts with breakfast, for example, and that members of his family who leave shortly after—his father or mother for work, older sisters and brothers for school—will show up later, when the afternoon shadows lengthen or darkness arrives.

The school day organizes itself more or less naturally around such events and needs as arriving and departing, morning and afternoon, food and rest, quiet and active times, indoor and outdoor activity. Typical daily schedules—one for a full-day program, the other for a half-day program—are given here. Both are guides, to be adapted by the preschool director and teacher to their purposes.

SUGGESTED DAILY PROGRAM
(Prekindergarten Teacher's Guide, Dayton Public Schools, Dayton Ohio)

A.M.

8:00	Staff planning
8:40	Greeting children at the door
	Self-chosen activities
9:30	Snack time
9:45	Story hour in small groups
10:05	Outdoor play—walks and sensorimotor training
10:35	Rest
10:50	Music and rhythms and sensorimotor training
11:10	Language development
11:30	Science or math experiences
11:45	Preparation for dismissal

P.M.

1:00	Greeting children at the door
	Self-chosen activities
1:45	Language development
2:00	Music and rhythms, science or math activities
2:15	Snack
	Rest
2:45	Outdoor play and sensorimotor training
3:00	Story time in small groups
3:15	Dismissal for children
3:15–	
3:30	Planning and evaluation for staff

SUGGESTED HALF-DAY PROGRAM
(Project HEAD START Daily Program II)

Morning		**Afternoon**
8:45–9:15	Arrival and independent activity	12:45-1:15
9:15–9:30	First assembly	1:15–1:30

9:30–9:45	Nourishment, story	1:30–2:30
9:45–10:45	First work period	2:30–2:45
10:45–11:00	Exercises, gymnastics, marching	2:45–3:00
11:00–11:50	Second work period	3:00–3:50
11:50–12:00	Final assembly	3:50–4:00
12:00	Go home	4:00

It should be stressed again that young children feel lost and uncomfortable in groups that teen-agers would consider small; to a preschooler, a group of fifteen might be a mob, and while he may enjoy singing for awhile with a group that size, it might be much too large for him to learn in comfortably.

Soon after entering a preschool, children will show a tendency to group themselves for certain activities, varying in number with the kind of play in which they are engaged. Provided that these informal groupings do not exclude the same youngsters again and again, the teacher should learn to work *with* them rather than impose her own group preferences.

Beyond the general scheduling necessitated by arrivals and departures, lunchtime, etc., the preschool teacher needs to develop more specific forms of planning for learning. Learning goals need to be identified with the needs of the children the program is serving. Normally, goals would be listed under the general headings numbers, science, language, social studies, etc., and would relate to the general objectives of the program. Examples of stated learning goals could be as follows. These curriculum learning goals for numbers are identified in the *Handbook for Prekindergarten and Kindergarten Teachers,* Cheshire Public Schools, Cheshire, Connecticut (1969, pp. 41-43).

NUMBERS

Basic Concepts

Mathematics is somewhat like a game in that rules set up conditions which are the basis for mathematical systems of thought.

Mathematics has a vocabulary of its own which must be mastered in understanding the following concepts:

Size	Fractional parts
Quantity	Terms of problem solving
Placement	Spatial relationships
Measurement	Shape
Money	Sets

The kindergarten child exists in a concrete world; therefore, concrete manipulative materials will fit his world and will present mathematical ideas at his level of understanding. From the concrete, the child will move to the abstract.

Opportunities within Total Program

We subscribe to the philosophy of "exposure." Application of number concepts should be meaningful; e.g., scoring games, counting for different purposes, measuring. Many situations afford good opportunities in an experience curriculum.

I. NUMBER CONCEPTS
    A. Value
       1. Number 1–10
    B. Symbols
       1. Numerals 1–10
    C. Sequence
       1. What comes before
       2. What comes after
       3. Number line
    D. Set
       1. Collection of things, objects, ideas
II. COUNTING 1–10
    A. Ordinals—first-sixth
    B. Cardinals—whole numbers
III. RECOGNITION OF GEOMETRIC FORMS
    A. Circle
    B. Square
    C. Triangle
    D. Rectangle
    E. Diamond
IV. MEASUREMENT
    A. Time

    1. Calendar

    2. Clock

      (a) Hour

      (b) Half hour

  B. Liquid

    1. One cup

    2. One-half cup

    3. Quart

    4. Pint

    5. One-half pint

  C. Linear

    1. Foot

    2. Yard

  D. Quantity

    1. Dozen

    2. One-half dozen

V. MONEY

  A. Recognition

    1. Penny

    2. Nickel

    3. Dime

    4. Quarter

    5. Half dollar

    6. Dollar

  B. Counting

    1. Coins

  C. Values

    1. 10 pennies—1 dime

            —2 nickels

    Others as occasion demands

Vocabulary

The following vocabulary is only a suggested list. Some children may be able to understand all the words, while others will be limited in their understanding because of background or experience.

A. Addition and Subtraction Terms and Symbols

1. Answer
2. Problem
3. Count
4. Add (put together or combine)
5. Subtract (take away)
6. Number line
7. Numeral vs. number
8. Set
9. Addend
10. Sum

$$\begin{array}{cc} \text{addend} & \text{sum} \\ +\ \underline{\text{addend}} & -\ \underline{\text{addend}} \\ \text{sum} & \text{addend} \end{array}$$

11. Number sentence = equation

B. Size and Amount Terms
1. More—Less
2. Big—Little
3. Long—Short
4. Large—Small
5. Many—Few
6. Heavy—Light
7. High—Low
8. Tall—Short
9. All—Enough—Some—None (not any)
10. Full—Empty

C. Comparative Terms—ex.: big, bigger, biggest

Above terms *(B)* used in comparative fashion; e.g., greater than, less than

D. Spatial Terms
1. Under—Over
2. Bottom—Top
3. First—Last
4. High—Low
5. Middle
6. Above—Below
7. Far—Near
8. In front of—Behind
9. Following—Leading
10. Begin—End

11. Beside
12. Around
13. Left—Right
14. Down—Up

E. *Measurement Tools*
　1. Ruler
　2. Tape measure
　3. Yardstick
　4. Thermometer
　5. Calendar
　6. Clock
　7. Cup
　8. Spoon

F. *Measurement— terms relative to tools*
　1. Long
　2. Short
　3. Empty
　4. Full
　5. Pair
　6. Cupful
　7. Spoonful
　8. Temperature
　9. Freezing
　10. Boiling

G. *Form*
　1. Circle
　2. Square
　3. Round
　4. Straight
　5. Rectangle
　6. Line
　7. Hole

H. *Time Terms*
　1. Day
　2. Today—Tomorrow
　3. Yesterday
　4. Night
　5. Last night

If you categorize activities into groups such as "social development," you might be making sense to parents and other teachers, but children grasp more meaningful descriptions such as "helping out around home."

6. Morning
7. Noon
8. Afternoon
9. Evening
10. Hour
11. Minute—Second
12. Month
13. Year
14. Fast
15. Slow

Finally, if preschool activities are to be more than a mere series of fragmentary experiences, they must be organized to give the youngster some sort of focus around which he can orient his work-play. It is not enough to lump these activities under such curricular categories as "science" or "numbers"; these are for the guidance of the staff and parents. Activities must also be grouped in categories that make sense to a child and show a clear relation to his experience and daily life.

One way of doing this is to devise a set of units, such as "Living in the Home," "Zoo Animals," "The Farm," "Safety," and "Eating Habits." *(Kindergarten Resource Units,* listed in the bibliography, is a good source for detailed planning ideas around such topics [Roanoke City Schools, 1968].) Properly organized, such units would cut across several curriculum categories and include learning goals from the different categories. The time at which units are introduced during the year can be important; some can be generated by the changing seasons of the year, interest of children, etc. Certainly, no unit should be continued after children have lost interest.

The following is a suggested activities chart as an instruction to teachers from the *Handbook for Prekindergarten and Kindergarten Teachers,* Cheshire, Connecticut (1969 pp. 63-67).

BREAKDOWN OF ACTIVITIES BY MONTHS

The following breakdown of activities by months is incorporated to provide suggestions for concrete planning, drawing on the basic concepts and contents of the curriculum guides. The list is compiled from the actual programs of Cheshire kindergarten teachers. The list is flexible, of course. Activities may be added or conducted at a period other than when scheduled. Not all topics could possibly be covered by one teacher in one classroom in a school year.

At the beginning of the year, blanket field-trip permission is obtained from parents for excursions within walking distance of the school.

SEPTEMBER AND OCTOBER

Topic	Trips, Visitors, Special Projects
I. Getting Acquainted Orientation	Tour of school building
A. People	
1. New friends	Introduction to school personnel
2. School personnel	
B. Places	Neighborhood walk
1. School plant	

C. Safety   Visit from state trooper (child's father)
    1. En route to school
    (a) Bus
    (b) Walking
    2. On playground—in building
    3. Fire drill

II. Summer Fun
    A. Travel
    B. Transportation
    C. Activities
    D. Clothing
    E. People met
    F. Food eaten

III. House and Family (see   Walks to nearby families to see kittens
    curriculum guide)   and new baby

IV. Fall Season   Watching favorite tree—record
    A. Clothing   changes from September to June
    B. Weather   Making applesauce
    C. Environmental changes   Trip to Cheshire Park
    D. Outdoor activities

V. Holidays
    A. Fire Prevention   Visit from Smokey the Bear
    B. Columbus Day   Party
    C. Hallowe'en   Parade   (administrative decision)

VI. Introduction of Color Concepts   Making cupcakes for Halloween
    A. Nature (Relate to all areas of   Collecting for UNICEF for trick or
    curriculum)   treat (administrative decision)

NOVEMBER AND DECEMBER

I. Indians   "Popcorn Party"—Indians and Pilgrims
    A. Tribes   First Thanksgiving Party
    B. Travel   Making cranberry sauce
    C. Homes
    D. Clothing
    E. Daily living
    F. Communications

II. Pilgrims
    A. Customs
    B. Culture

III. Harvest
    A. Kinds of food   Trip to Bishop Farms
    B. Preservation   Trip to Hickory Hill Farm

IV. Winter
    A. Environmental changes
    B. Hibernation
    C. Indoor and outdoor activities
V. Holidays
    A. Veterans' Day   Visit *from* service man
    B. Thanksgiving—past and
        present   Trip to local nursery
    C. Christmas   Visit *from* Santa
                          Community service project
                          Walk to town to see decorations in
                            store windows

JANUARY AND FEBRUARY

I. Winter   Science experiment—melting snow
    A. Weather   Making mittens
    B. Clothing   Listening to radio for weather
    C. Outdoor activities   broadcast
    D. Effects on transportation and   Looking for animal tracks
        communications   Walking in snow
    E. Animal life   Planting bean seeds and narcissus
    F. Indoor planting   bulbs
    G. Health   Visit from Dentist or Hygienist—
                          Dental Health Week

II. Birds in Winter
    A. Types   Making and supplying bird feeder—
    B. Care of   making "bird menu"

III. Holidays
    A. Valentine's Day   Delivering valentines—Valentine's
    B. Lincoln's Birthday   Day Party
    C. Washington's Birthday
    D. Presidents—past—present

IV. Postal System
    A. Delivery   Visit to Post Office
    B. Home Address   Building Post Office in classroom

V. Shoe store
    A. Need   Constructing store and supplying boxes
    B. Variety   of different sized shoes
    C. Supply and demand   Dramatic play—fitting and buying

VI. Baker
    A. Supplier   Making and baking cake
    B. Goods and services

MARCH AND APRIL

I. Spring
    A. Seeds and bulbs   Planting in room
    B. Weather   Visit to greenhouse
    C. Environmental changes   Making pinwheels—kites
                           Walk to see what wind does
                           Observing weather vane

    D. Baby animals   Trip to Brewerton Brothers Game Farm
                           Bringing baby chicks, lambs, bunnies to classroom
                           Trip to Hall's Hatchery

II. Holidays   Making Easter baskets as community
    A. Easter   service project
    B. St. Patrick's Day   Visit from native of Ireland

III. Holland
    A. Windmills   Showing of slides taken by parent
    B. Tulips
    C. Traditional clothing

IV. Store
    A. Merchant's role   Trip to supermarket to buy doughnuts
    B. Goods and services   for snack time
    C. Monetary exchange

V. Dairy
    A. Source of supply for milk Visit to Greenbacker's Dairy
       products
    B. Method of production   Making butter in classroom

MAY AND JUNE

I. Holidays

    A. Mother's Day   Making gifts and cards
    B. Memorial Day   Parade within school

C. Father's Day
D. Flag Day

II. Season
    A. Plants—wild and cultivated   Making terrarium
    B. Birds   Planting annuals
    C. Weather changes   Walk for signs of warm weather
         Making May baskets—delivering to neighbors
         Performing Maypole dance

III. Tall Grass Zoo
    A. Species   Bringing snakes, tadpoles, insects,
    B. Care of   turtles, butterflies to classroom

IV. Circus: vs. Carnival
    A. Wild animals   Putting on show
    B. Varied jobs
    C. Precision of jobs
    D. Comparison
V. The Farm
    A. Animals and babies
    B. Machinery

IV. Pets (see curriculum guide) •   Visits of special pets to school

VII. Approaching Summer Vacation
    A. Safety   Visit from policeman
    B. Activities   Visit from member of recreation and
    C. Trips planned   park commission

Topics such as these furnish both a focus and a good deal of flexibility. They can involve all kinds of materials, media, activities; the ways and means of exploring them are limited only by the ingenuity and imagination of both teacher and children. Indeed, the children themselves should as much as possible participate in the selection and planning of various "projects" and activities within broad topic areas as well as in the selection of the topics themselves.

A second advantage of such topics is that they cut across the so-called content or subject categories that serve as the organizing principle in much later schooling. What the young child needs to learn is not content or information, but skills such as sensory discrimination, control over small and large muscle activity and coordination, language facility, and so on. And he can develop these skills around almost any subject.

It must always be kept in mind that the purpose of planning, scheduling, preparation—as of all preschool education—is to help the child gain greater competence and control over his own affairs. They are a kind of scaffolding that must never be mistaken for substance.

RECORD KEEPING

Learning as much as possible about the child is a *sine qua non* to helping the child learn as much as possible. Careful and complete records of each child's programs are indispensable in developing an accurate idea of a child's needs, in informing parents and enlisting their support.

The teacher needs, first of all, to find out all she can about each child *before* he enters preschool. She should, for example, know something about his health and developmental history (what diseases has he had? any physical problems?), his home background (has he watched much TV? have his parents read to him a lot? is he an only child? what is the education and economic background of his parents?), his personality, and so on.

The teacher can then build upon this information, carefully recording as much as she can about a child's home environment, his mental progress, his personal characteristics, his relations with others, and the like. A simple checklist showing the teacher's observations of some of these traits can be developed.

But the records on each child should consist of more than numbers and check marks; it is also useful for the teacher to record descriptive remarks and anecdotes that convey something of the living child. A notation that one child seems especially interested in painting, or that another seems most happy and contented when she is with other girls, provides the discerning teacher with ideas for future class activities and with clues to individual learning styles.

Every teacher must guard against the danger of developing fixed ideas and stereotypes about a child. Children are uncanny in aping the image of themselves that they see reflected in the eyes and attitudes of others—especially adults who have some authority over them. The world is full of people who "can't" do things because, as far back as they can remember, they were told they "couldn't" do them. Teacher expectations and attitudes have an enormous influence—almost the force of self-fulfilling prophecies—upon the achievements of young children.

One of the great advantages, to the conscientious teacher, of trying to keep a living and running record of each child is that it requires her to continually test her previous impressions of each child as well as her responses to his needs. In trying to catch the changing picture of each child as he changes, she constantly forces herself to look anew at each child and at her picture of him. Certainly, information recorded along with the observations of the teacher should be discussed with parents from time to time to help establish a continued positive overlap of information and activities between home and school.

HOME AND SCHOOL

A considerable body of research tells us that the influence of home and parents clearly exceeds that of the school, and child-development specialists generally agree that parental involvement is essential to an effective preschool program. At a minimum, teachers must be able to explain to parents what the preschool program is intended to accomplish in easily understandable layman's terms, and parents must support program goals.

Beyond this shared understanding, a number of routine procedures are indicated to enable parents and teachers to exchange information about each child. The teacher should meet each child's parents upon his admission to the school and should have an individual session with them each term to review the child's progress. Parents should be invited to the school to observe their youngsters while the program is in session, to deepen their understanding of what the school is doing and why. Parents may be encouraged to assist in the classroom and to accompany children on field trips.

However, there is a much more interesting concept of parental involvement that focuses on the educational possibilities inherent in the home. Parents do many good things instinctively and purely out of love for and interest in their children. But they could do many more good things, developmentally stimulating things, for their children if an imaginative, insightful teacher showed them how to *use* the "curriculum" hidden in the daily activities of any family. Such use of developmental possibilities in the home, moreover, need not be restricted to special times when a parent puts aside all other tasks to devote to a child; the possibilities are there throughout the day if a parent learns how to recognize them and "harvest" them.

For example, most parents buy their preschool children picture books; from time to time they page through the book and ask their youngsters to identify oranges, apples, and so forth. This is an entirely sound practice. But reality is usually more interesting than the representation of reality, and a supermarket can be a much more stimulating place to look for apples and oranges than the pages of a book. No mother would ask a four-year-old, "Get me a chuck roast," but she can ask her child to find a familiar fruit, or the aisle with the cereals. Small-number exercises can be built into shopping: "We need four lemons. Why don't you put them in the cart? That's one. Put another in. That makes two. Put another..." Similarly, preparing food, washing and ironing clothes, and even performing the drudgeries of housekeeping can supply opportunities for the naming of objects, the grouping of like things ("can you pick all the socks out of the laundry and put them in a separate pile?"), the measuring of quantities, and other activities which stimulate the child's development and give him a chance to exercise (and show off, to his most appreciative audience) his growing skills.

Many parents do this sort of thing by instinct, without thinking twice about it or realizing that they are performing truly educational work. The interesting challenge facing preschool teachers, now that the importance of "parental involvement" has been recognized, is to help all parents do well what a few do by intuition. How can lessons be distilled from the home? How can the insights that a preschool teacher gains, through training and experience, be adapted for use by parents?

Therefore, instead of focusing on what the *school* does during evening meetings with parents, teachers should consider shifting the theme of occasional lectures by guest speakers, group discussions, interviews with parents, and other "involvement" activities to the educational significance of what *parents* do.

Parental involvement is a two-way street in the professional sense, too. Most preschool teachers will encounter at least one precocious, developmentally advanced child in the course of a year. Why does the child seem to be ahead of other children his age? A visit with the child's mother, a frank confession of admiration for her child-rearing practices and of interest in finding out what she does that works so well, will not only gain the teacher a friend but may provide her with a teaching strategy that can be used in the preschool classroom with other children for years to come.

THE PHYSICAL ENVIRONMENT

The physical environment, like every other aspect of early learning, must center around the child. The furniture must be of a size and weight that enable the child to handle and use it with ease; yet it must be sturdy enough to stand a good deal of tough wear. Everything ought to be within the child's reach, and, so far as possible, within his capacity to move, to lift, to manage.

In general, the atmosphere ought to be one of neither excessive neatness nor bewildering chaos, but of ordered abundance. The child ought to have a sense that this is a great place for him to be: on the one hand it is filled with all sorts of interesting things and, on the other, it is something he can cope with physically, mentally, and emotionally.

The indoor area is best divided into different sections or alcoves, each containing a different activity or related group of activities—such as for creative play, music, water play, and so on. The precise number of activities will depend largely on the space and equipment available as well as on the number of children. These areas should be open to a common center or accessway so that any child can move easily and freely from one to another without interfering with anyone else.

Some activities are quieter than others; some involve more physical activity; some involve individual work and some involve small groups; some are messy and some not. These factors must be taken into account when arranging the room. Obviously, it is not a good idea to put the woodworking or drama area next to the children's library center.

There are some very specific ways in which the physical environment can and ought to serve as a learning experience. Objects of a single kind, for example, can be stored together; the very process of taking them out and putting them back requires the child to make certain comparisons and contrasts, to distinguish between objects that belong together and those that do not. It is possible to construct shelves in such a way that the child can store the same items—blocks, for example—according to different criteria of size, shape, color, and so on. Shelves for blocks can be distinguished from other shelves by a sign that contains a picture of a block and the word *block*—thus stressing the importance of symbols, the relation between symbols and things, and the relation between pictorial and verbal symbols.

As much as possible, the indoor room should open to the outdoors so that the child can move as easily between indoor and outdoor activity as he can between different indoor activities. The outdoor area should be equipped for imaginative and active play; abstract or neutral forms seem to be best—since the less recognizable they are, the more scope they offer to the child's own inventiveness. (Much of this equipment can be made.) The outdoor area is, of course, a great place for sand and water play, building blocks, animal hutches, gardens and plants, greenhouses, and just plain running around.

The bibliography lists a number of books on arranging the physical environment for early learning.

Activity Centers

$\mathbf{T}$he preceding parts briefly describe the importance of early childhood education, outline the problem of the match, and suggest a perspective for the practitioner to follow in designing a program that relates educational goals to child readiness, and to preschool materials and activities. As with curriculum at any level of education, rationale should precede program—that is, before deciding *what* students should do, the teacher should decide *why* they should do it by relating to the needs of the children.

Part III moves into the establishment of "activity centers" and the relationship of the centers to the "educational" programs for preschool children. Each category of activities has an instructional *intent* as well as *content,* and the teacher should try to bear the distinction in mind as he or she works with the children. The instructional content of a unit of water play, for example, may involve a great deal of pouring water back and forth into vessels of various sizes. Entertaining as they may be—and these activities have been chosen at least partially because they do keep children interested—the instructional intent may be to demonstrate that no matter what size or shape the vessel in which it is contained, one pint of water remains one pint of water.

Several lessons can be drawn from this activity by a perceptive teacher. Conservation of mass, for one; training in perception—a coupling of the brain and the senses—to make correct judgments despite physical appearances, for another. *In any event the instruc-*

tional intent should be related to the learning goals of ECE and the activity centers can be used as interesting tools for children to meet or understand the goals.

The nature of the instructional intent will differ from activity to activity, lending itself to considerations of quantity in one, to quality in another. In art, for example, the imaginative teacher might set several student compositions side by side and ask which picture seems warm, which seems cold, which animal seems happier, and why. From there the discussion might lead into the emotional effects of certain colors and into experiments with masses of black, red, or yellow to create purposely an impression of warmth, happiness, lightness, or weight. The shape of a line can make a great difference: changing an upturned mouth into a downturned one changes mood from pleasure to gloom. What difference does the shape of an eyebrow make? Also, different activity centers may be used to cover the same instructional intent, depending on the interest, maturation, and learning sytle of the student. Obviously, all children *do not* participate in similar activities at the same time nor do they have similar instructional intents.

Again, these suggestions are not exhaustive. They are merely a sampling, intended to carry forward the purpose of this book by helping the practitioner understand how instructional goals can be translated into instructional practice, with proper student involvement. The teacher should read them not to memorize them but to stimulate his or her own imagination and to help adapt to him or her own purpose the hundreds of other ideas contained in the books listed in the bibliography or available to him or her from other sources in meeting the needs of the students.

Creative Play

There is no really satisfactory way to describe play, let alone define it. In general, it is anything done without some strictly utilitarian purpose and without coercion. Mark Twain once wrote that "play consists of whatever a body is not obliged to do"— which is acceptable enough, except that the young child is, in a real sense, *obliged* to play. For the child, play is not simply a pleasant if peripheral pastime, but very largely the major reason for living. The child plays not to *avoid* reality but to *encounter* it. Play is the idiom by which children express themselves and the avenue through which they explore, experience, and interpret the world around them. It is the way they work—and the primary language through which they learn.

The young child approaches things largely on the sensory and motor level. He or she needs to come into contact with things—to feel and see and smell them over and over again—before really getting to know them. A good many mistakes in preschool education stem from our tendency to forget this need. We often overestimate a young child's ability to think like an adult, to approach reality on an abstract, symbolic, and highly verbal level. And we underestimate—and undervalue—the child's ability to grow and learn in largely nonverbal, concrete, and presymbolic ways.

Piaget has observed that "you cannot teach [young children] concepts verbally; you must use a method founded on activity." The preschool child has only recently started using language, and it still remains for him or her a largely inadequate, clumsy instrument of learning. It can help illuminate what the child already knows by other means, but it is a poor guide to the unfamiliar and the unknown. Language cannot be neglected, but until

49

a child's language skills are more fully developed and the child is able to function effectively on an abstract and verbal level, his or her most important learning must occur—or at least begin—in nonverbal ways. Consequently, the preschool program must place a heavy stress on play as an instructional device, adapting it to the objectives of the curriculum and the interests of the children.

According to the standard developmental scenario, the child will progress from predominantly solitary play to parallel play (playing alongside of, but not *with,* others) to genuinely cooperative and interpersonal play. The child tends to enter fully into cooperative play around the age of five. But in this matter as in all other aspects of "standard development," the teacher should be aware that each child will work his or her own variations upon this sequence. Too often, warn Hartley, Frank, and Goldenson in *Understanding Children's Play* (1952, p. 125), "preschool and kindergarten groups seem to be planned on the assumption that all young children are, or should be, constantly gregarious. They must play together, eat together, and sleep together, with little cognizance taken of the very real service of growth that solitude can offer."

FUNCTIONS OF PLAY

A child's play is a unified and unitary experience; despite the best attempts of various experts to do so, it does not yield easily to efforts to divide it into neat little parts. One authority, for example, distinguishes between three kinds or functions of play, another between four, another between six, and yet another between eight.

It will serve our purpose to say simply that the child learns through play in at least four ways:

1. *The child learns about physical things* through manipulative and motor play of all sorts. By working with blocks, manipulation toys, sand and water, and the like, the child learns about the shapes, dimensions, and conceptual properties of things. The child discovers their likenesses and differences, sorting them out and classifying them according to color, size, and weight. The child finds out what he or she can and cannot do with them.

2. *The child learns about the world of people* through dramatic and other kinds of joint play. By acting out various "roles" such as doctor, father, mother, nurse, policeman, and fireman, the child learns about the different relations people have with each other in society. By playing with other children in the block corner, at the water faucet, or wherever, the child learns about himself or herself in relation to others—about the need for give and take, taking turns, sharing. The child learns that others may have different points of view, feelings, and the like.

3. *The child learns about himself or herself.* In dramatic play, the child acts out his or her fears, frustrations, and feelings. In art, in water play, in block play, the child works these emotions out by expressing them in nonverbal forms. With every new experience, the child encounters a new aspect of himself or herself; every new skill, every new accomplishment represents a new discovery, for it is something that was not there before.

4. *The child develops physically.* The child develops and coordinates small and large muscle movements through active participation in both indoor and outdoor activities and by using proper equipment.

DRAMATIC PLAY

In dramatic play, the child assumes and acts out some imagined role or series of roles, either alone or together with others. Dramatic play can occur anywhere, anytime: at the block corner, outdoors, wherever and whenever the child is free to engage in it and feels like doing so. It probably advances a child's total development in a more critical way than any other kind of play.

Hartley, Frank, and Goldenson (1952) list eight major functions of dramatic play:

1. It enables children to try on adult roles for size. They can thus understand what it is to be a mother or father by actually "becoming" a mother or father.

2. It permits them to play out their real selves in a more intense way. Most often this is a compulsive kind of role playing: in extreme cases, the child engages in it because he feels incapable of doing anything else (the child, for example, who is "submissive" in both play and real life).

Are they astronauts on their way to Saturn, or business partners in a candy factory? Through role-acting and joint play, these children are developing ideas about how people relate to one another in the world they are growing into.

3. It serves as a reflection of the child's home life.

4. It enables children to fulfill in fantasy desires they cannot fulfill in fact.

5. It gives children an acceptable outlet for expressing "forbidden impulses," for trying to come to grips with a host of feelings that they cannot deal with in real life because they are not allowed to express them.

6. It permits children to explore new aspects of themselves by reversing their real life roles. The submissive child, for example, may play a dominating parent; the aggressive child may play a weak and dependent infant.

7. It mirrors a child's personal and social growth.

8. It offers children, in general, a kind of laboratory, a safe setting, for working out personal problems and experimenting with new possibilities.

There is, then, no more vital or versatile preschool activity than dramatic play. It offers the child a uniquely personal and (for all the talk that is sometimes involved) essentially nonverbal means of communication, contact, and cooperation. It is an ideal medium through which children can move, in their own time and in their own way, from the predominantly egocentric focus that characterizes preschool children to the increasingly social viewpoint that older children are capable of.

The teacher can learn a great deal about a child by quietly watching him or her in dramatic play and by recording observations and impressions over a period of time. Although the roles and relations that children assume in dramatic play are fairly standard, each child has a way of performing those roles and engaging in those relations that is unique; the pattern of a child's dramatic play is like a signature or a fingerprint.

In dramatic play, children write their own script. But a variety of props can do a lot to stimulate their imaginations and open up different possibilities. Following are some suggestions for setting the stage.

DRAMATIC PLAY (OR HOUSEKEEPING CORNER): Set aside one area of the room with screens, shelves, or other dividers. Equip it with child-size furniture and other materials that children can use to assume a range of roles: family roles such as father, mother and baby, as well as roles beyond the home such as mailman, fireman, milkman. A partial list might include dress-up clothes (for men as well as women), table, chairs, mirrors, kitchen and eating utensils, telephones, stove, refrigerator, sink, tool boxes, lunch boxes, briefcases, keys, billfolds, dolls, puppets, and so on.

OUTDOOR DRAMATIC PLAY: A lot of energetic dramatic play will take place outside in the playground. There, the best props are the simplest and the least specific: free-form sculptures, the sand box, planks and boards and sawhorses, crates and boxes of assorted sizes, wheelbarrows and bicycles and trucks, hollow building blocks, crawl tunnels, and so on.

BLOCK PLAY

Adults often forget that the power to "make" implies the power to "break." And they are disturbed by the unabashed joy children exhibit when they destroy something they have taken great pains to make (this is true of sand, clay, and other play materials as well).

But this so-called destructive play serves some valuable educational functions:

1. It is a safe outlet for hostile, aggressive feelings.

2. It is a way of exploring and expanding a child's limits. By destroying what he creates, the child (again in a safe situation) enlarges his sense of self-control, of power over the things he makes.

3. It is a way of getting things ready to begin building again. It is not the product he makes that is important but the process of making it. And he wants to go through that process again and again.

BLOCK CORNER: This requires a large floor area with adjacent shelves and storage areas for all sorts of blocks. There are basically two kinds of blocks: the large hollow building blocks and the smaller solid blocks. Both should be available in as much abundance and diversity as space will allow. You might also want to include boxes, boards, barrels, transportation toys, family figures, community figures, and animal figures.

Together with the other "natural" materials (sand, water, paper, clay), blocks constitute an important medium of play and learning in the preschool. They are easy to use; they have a diversity of uses (they can "be" anything and can be employed in a variety of activities); they are sturdy and clean; and they do not intimidate the child.

They are an unparalleled medium for allowing the child to grow in his or her own eyes. When the child builds airports, skyscrapers, and the like he or she is both cutting the adult world down to size and expanding his or her own sense of power. The child is coming to terms with the outside, outsize, and often overwhelming world of the adult.

In addition, blocks can be used to promote understanding of math concepts, dimensions, balance, and eye-hand coordination.

WATER PLAY

Water is probably the single most useful substance in the preschool inventory. It is easily available and infinitely malleable. It seems to hold an almost mystical allure for children. They can pour it, splash it, paint and wash with it, drink it, squeeze things in it, soak things in it, bathe in it, fill things with it, do almost anything in and with it. It stimulates children who are withdrawn and relaxes children who are too excited or aggressive. It is, on the whole, the substance that comes closest to being all things to all children.

Indeed, the value and attractiveness of several other basic preschool materials stem very largely from their association with water. Clay and mud are "wet earth." Finger and brush paints are "colored water." Sand is "dry water" that serves, in many experiments, as a satisfactory substitute for "wet" water.

Unfortunately, the appeal of water to children is often exceeded only by the aversion of teachers to it. It is, they say, altogether too messy. Children will splash it all over everything and everybody. And besides, what can you do with it?

Such teachers (and adults generally, especially parents) should observe that water seems to calm and interest adults much as it does children. Architects use splashing fountains and reflecting pools to break up otherwise oppressive expanses of concrete and glass; the fact that public areas in which pools and fountains are located so often have benches around them for sitting and peaceful contemplation suggests that water may have been man's first tranquilizer. No one knows precisely *why* water has this effect on humans, but it is important to recognize that it *does* and that water can be employed as an instructional device.

Because children find water so attractive and absorbing and because it can be put to so many uses, it seems to work better than any other material in increasing the attention span of children. They never tire of working with it, often repeating the same operation over and over again.

The Children's Museum in Boston offers an excellent water-play kit with materials and an illustrated booklet of suggested activities.

Whatever an adult's misgivings are about putting preschoolers in the vicinity of water, the water and the resulting water play can provide several worthwhile learning activities.

Children can substitute sand for water in many experiments. "Dry water" flows great through a funnel, just like the real stuff.

MATERIALS

INDOORS

Kitchen utensils of all kinds:
    Plastic and metal for
      measuring and pouring
    Sieves

Various size bowls, pans, aprons, mops, sponges, pails, funnels, pumps, tetrahedrons, test tubes, and syringes
Tubing of various sorts

OUTDOORS

In addition to the above materials, all of which can be used outdoors:
    Hoses
    Wading pools
    Buckets

Boats
Other wooden or plastic devices

ACTIVITIES

Indoors, the most convenient place for water play is probably in or near the "kitchen" area, with faucets installed over a large washtub-type sink. Children can work directly in the sink, out of a single large washtub, or out of separate small washbowls or basins on an area of the floor or on tables covered with waterproof material. Outdoors, almost anywhere will do as long as it does not interfere with other activities.

Water-play activities should be as free and spontaneous as possible—with more complex techniques and materials introduced as children seem ready for and receptive to them. You may need to set some limits so that, for example, one child doesn't bother another. But it is all too easy to overrestrict and overreact and to become terribly concerned about the exuberance children sometimes display during water play. Beyond the minimum limits necessary to protect the children and the premises, let them go. Mopping up is as much a part of water play as splashing around, and children like to do one just as much as the other.

Children can do more things with water than most adults can dream up. Here are some of them.

DISCOVER ITS NATURAL PROPERTIES: By turning the faucet in varying degrees, they feel the different pressures that running water can make on their hands. With their hands and fingers, they can change the nature and direction of the faucet stream: make it go into a container to the left or right, make it spread or spurt. They can make bubbles, waves, ripples, or splashes— each with a different sound—simply by doing different things with their hands.

DO SIMPLE EXPERIMENTS:
1. Pour water from container to container in different ways: from small into large, large into small, etc.; from one container to another (varying sizes) through a funnel; from a container into tubing with or without a funnel.
2. Make water go through sieves, strainers, paper cups, or plastic jars with holes in sides.
3. Use various vacuum techinques to fill and empty containers. Using a meat baster, for example, squeeze the bulb

to create a vacuum in cylinder; place into container of water; release bulb; and watch water climb up cylinder. Pull baster from water; squeeze water into container. Similar experiments can be performed with atomizers, squeeze bottles, or squirt bottles (window washing, hand lotion).

4. Measure different quantities of water with measuring cups and spoons or graduated tubes.

5. Paint with water: indoors on newspaper, colored paper, etc.; outdoors on concrete, sand, sidewalk, wood, etc.

6. Make soap bubbles: Add soap to water, stir to make bubbles, blow to create a current; and watch bubbles move along the water. Discuss why bubbles were formed.

7. Squeeze or soak up water with sponges and various kinds of cloth, noticing difference in weight when article is filled with water or empty of it.

8. Mix and dissolve various ingredients with water (hot, lukewarm, or cold), flour, sugar, food coloring, salad oil, alcohol, liquid soap, sand, salt, cornstarch, soda, etc.

Do More Elaborate Experiments:

1. Floating/sinking: Collect a number of small objects from room: plastic, wooden, cork, metal, rocks, seeds, feathers. See what happens when each is put in a container of water; see if it makes any difference what temperature the water is, or whether it is mixed with something (like soap, oil). Try to guess which will sink, which will float, and why.

2. Siphoning: Fill pail from large tank. Put a piece of tubing in tank and allow to fill up with water. Holding fingers over both openings, put one end in tank and other in smaller container, with the end in the smaller container lower than the other. Take fingers off both ends; water will siphon from tank into smaller and lower container.

Many of the siphoning and pouring techniques can be used, along with mopping and sponging, during clean-up time. All these activities can be done outside with tubs, hoses, streams, rain, puddles, and so on. The outcomes and processes of these activities should be reviewed and discussed with the children.

PHYSICAL PLAY

For children, physical play is much more than just becoming strong and healthy—although that in itself is obviously important. In a real sense, the child *is* his or her body. Learning who they are and what they can do is largely a question of learning about their bodies and what their bodies can do.

Children use their bodies and develop some physical skill, usually involving the small muscles, in every preschool activity. But they also need to engage in physical activity for its own sake—especially to test their large-muscle skills and strength by running, jumping, climbing, balancing, and spinning.

OUTDOORS AND IN: Outdoors is obviously the ideal place for the more active and intense kinds of physical play, and the preschool playground should have the equipment as well as enough sheer space—at least 70 square feet per child—to stimulate as many different kinds of physical movement as possible: jungle gym, balance and jumping boards, ropes, ladders, rubber tires, inner tubes, balls, beanbags, shovels, brooms, slides, wheelbarrows, tricycles, sandboxes, paint brushes, boxes and crates, and the like.

None of this equipment needs to be elaborate and expensive; some of it can be improvised. What matters is that it all be sturdy and safe.

Too often, indoors and outdoors are regarded as mutually exclusive domains. But when the weather is good, there is no reason why painting, water play, and the like cannot take place outdoors. And when the weather is too cold or wet for outdoor activity, there is every reason to let children enjoy some robust physical play indoors. If at all possible, some indoor space should be equipped for that kind of play: with ladders, ropes, floors marked for hopscotch, areas open for rope skipping, and perhaps balance and jumping boards.

Though elaborate calisthenics and organized physical exercises should generally be avoided, children can learn a good deal through brief periods of group physical activity—no more than five or ten minutes a day. Most children of preschool age obtain as much physical exercise as they need through sheer rambunctiousness. The problem for preschool teachers is not to ensure that children get enough physical activity but to channel their energies in ways that will not endanger the teacher's own mental health, and to provide youngsters with another outlet for learning experiences.

The bibliography identifies a number of helpful sources.

Art and Sculpture

More than most other forms of preschool activity, art and sculpture enable children to express themselves by making their own mark on the world. In the process, while they strengthen their sense of visual discrimination and their abilities to manipulate things with their fingers, while they explore the possibilities of color and shape and various materials, they also discover a good deal about themselves.

They do, that is, if teachers are careful not to impose their adult standards of what constitutes "art." Children's skill with numbers, language, and the use of their muscles for running and jumping, and in most other aspects of the preschool curriculum, can be evaluated by objective measurements. Art and sculpture, however, are primarily areas in which youngsters should be free to express their own creativity in any way they please; many a youngster's interest in making his or her own art has been stifled by a teacher who coaxed the drawing of "recognizable" objects (recognizable to the teacher, that is) or who provided coloring books that do most of the child's creative thinking for him.

Until about the age of seven, children are as much interested in the *process* of art as they are in the *product*. At most, the product—whether painting, mobile, or collage—is a mirror of the process, and youngsters lose interest in what they have done soon after they complete it. One "process" is over, and it is time to begin another.

As preschool youngsters mold and scribble and paint, they are doing at least four things:

    1. They are developing various kinds of skills; increasing

manual dexterity, improving their visual discrimination and sense of touch.

2. They are building up what Rhoda Kellogg, in *The Psychology of Children's Art* (1967), calls a "basic repertoire" of patterns, shapes, and designs that enable them to do progressively more elaborate and intricate things.

3. They are becoming much more aware of colors, shapes, forms, and textures in their world—an awareness that carries over into science, math, and language activities.

4. They are expressing—though without being aware of it—their feelings in a personal, nonverbal, constructive form.

In brief, they are both developing and discovering themselves through action. Because art is one of relatively few human activities that allows people to act without subjecting themselves to standards of "right" and "wrong," the preschool teacher must take care not to stifle this channel for personal expression by telling children what to draw or in other ways restricting their creativity. If the result is a mess, that's all right; the point is, it's *his* or *her* mess.

One value of art in preschool accrues to the teacher rather than the children. Adults tend to approve of children's art when they can see in a painting, drawing, or shape a form that they recognize—a house, an animal, a tree. Most of us, however, are blind to the artistic appeal of interesting combinations of color and form when they are totally abstract—i.e., when they seem to represent nothing whatever. By withholding judgment on children's productions and by staunchly forbidding themselves to push children to draw something they can recognize, teachers may rediscover an interest in color and shape, pure and simple, that comes naturally to children but is frequently lost by adults.

Because teachers may be pressured by parents for art and sculpture that *they* can recognize, it may be helpful to know that most children do not enter into the pictorial stage of art—that point at which their drawings begin to look like things—until they are four or five years old. Before that, they progress from simple scribbling—apparently aimless lines—to patterns in which,

Freed from the constraints of right and wrong, a child can engage in a form of "instant" self-expression through the processes of art.

Children generally don't produce recognizable forms (at least adults are incapable of recognizing them) until around the age of four or five.

for example, circles will be crossed. Undecipherable as most of these scribbles and patterns are, they appear with striking regularity and sequence in the drawings and paintings of children at certain ages no matter what their socioeconomic background or even their national origin.

The teacher's job, in art as in other activities, is to respond to the child's needs as he or she expresses them. The teacher should be ready to demonstrate a techinque—finger painting, for example, or the design of a mobile—if a child expresses an interest in learning something new; after the demonstration, however, and an invitation to the youngster to try his or her own hand at it, the teacher should drop the subject rather than try to prescribe the content of an art activity. Indeed, the only rules that teachers should set for art are rules for themselves.

"Children who are left alone to draw what they like," writes Kellogg, "develop a store of knowledge which enables them to reach their final stage of self-taught art. . . .Most children, however, lose interest in drawing after the first few years of school because they are not given this chance to develop freely" (1967,

p. 17). What is true of drawing is true also of every other form of art and sculpture.

DRAWING AND PAINTING

The best way to help children draw is to give them lots of paper (vary the kinds, sizes, textures), different kinds of large crayons, pencils, and pens, and let them go. Later, if the children seem interested, you might want to introduce them to more specialized forms of drawing (stenciling, for example), but these should never be substituted for free drawing.

Painting, naturally enough, requires more organization. The first thing is to prepare for the mess. For the children, the messy part of painting is not, as it often is for the adult, a necessary evil. It is, to be sure, an inevitable part of their process of learning greater and finer control over their own movements, but it is also part of the fun. They should be given a good

What is very neat one minute will probably be a mess the next. Protect table tops, floors, and, if necessary, the child from what are bound to be the natural consequences of his or her exuberant involvement with the arts.

DRAWING AND PAINTING MATERIALS

	Improvised	*Store-bought*
Paper sizes: 18 x 24 inch and 12 x 18 inch—no smaller	Shelf paper Brown/white wrapping paper Newspaper Magazines Waxed paper	Finger-painting paper Construction paper Art/drawing paper (smooth/rough; medium/heavy weight) Manila paper Newsprint
Paper substitutes	Oil cloth Smooth, coated table tops	
Brushes	Small, cut paint brushes Toothbrushes	Easel brushes (⅜ inch, ½ inch, ¾ inch long-handled; wide, stiff bristles)
Paints (*all colors:* red, yellow, blue, black, white, purple, etc.)	Finger paint Home-made paint	Finger paint Liquid/powder tempera Poster paint
Drawing materials	Ink (India, regular) Large pencils Felt markers (all colors) Large crayons Chalk (all colors)	Lecturers chalk (various colors, soft) Compressed charcoal Drawing pencils (6B) Wax crayons
Miscellaneous materials	Easels Glass, plastic containers Paper cups Pails, buckets Trays Smocks (old shirts) Straws Screens String Sponges Tables Water	Cotton balls Stamp pad Vegetables, fruit Squeeze bottles Atomizer, spray gun Roller

deal of latitude to make mistakes and messes without feeling that it is bad or naughty. So get out the newspapers, cover the table and floor, and cover the children with smocks of some sort (old adult shirts, shower curtains, sheets, plastic aprons). Have water and sponges nearby.

If you are using easels, get them ready beforehand—with paper clipped on. The floor or a table will do as well as an easel and presents less of a dripping problem. Baby-food jars are good for storing, and muffin tins for mixing paints. Have a lot of good stiff brushes available so that the children can use different ones for different colors.

Make cleaning up as much a part of the activity as the painting—a form of water play. (You might experiment with involving children in the preparation as well—although this is time-consuming.)

Finger painting is also a kind of water play—with many of the same therapeutic and expressive functions. Children enjoy it the same way they enjoy making mud pies. A note of caution: Keep your eye on the rare child who doesn't welcome the chance to mess around with finger paints, for this child probably needs it most. Often such a child has been so inhibited by strictures at home against dirt and mess that he or she regards finger painting as something "bad." The child should not be pushed but should by all means be encouraged to try it.

ACTIVITIES
1. *Drawing*
    a.   Paper—drawing paper, newsprint, etc.
    b.   Crayons, pencils, chalk, charcoal
    c.   Free scribbling, etc.
    d.   Fixatives for charcoal and chalk—hair spray—to prevent smudging
2. *Crayon/chalk rubbing—extra materials: screens, grills, bark, coins, etc.*
    a.   Place paper over object.
    b.   Crayon or draw with chalk over the entire area, showing outline of object.
3. *Crayon etching—extra materials: spoon, scissors, needle, etc.*
    a.   'Cover paper with different crayon colors.

      b.   Cover this design with black crayon or ink.

      c.   With edge of spoon, scissors, needle, "etch" out lines, design showing the colors underneath.

4. *Stencil*

      a.   Cut stencil (paper, cardboard, etc.) to various shapes and sizes.

      b.   Rub heavy layer of chalk around edges of stencil.

      c.   Attach stencil(s) to paper.

      d.   Rub chalk off stencil onto paper with cloth.

      e.   Remove stencil and outline remains (spray).

5. *Finger painting*

      a.   Prepare glossy surface (paper or smooth table) by wetting completely—with sponge (or dip paper in water).

      b.   Dip hands in prepared paint (different colors in jars, containers) and spread paint over entire area.

      c.   Using fingers (hands, elbows, etc.), make designs.

      d.   Allow to dry (hang on clothesline).

      e.   Press on reverse side with warm iron.

      f.   (Variations: Follow steps 1–3, then place clean piece of paper on top of wet paint and press down; remove and dry—mono-printing.)

6. *Poster painting*

      a.   Prepare surface (easel, table), paper, brushes, paints.

      b.   Free painting (combine with crayon—wax resist).

      c.   Rinse brushes to keep colors distinct (water jar handy).

      d.   Hang finished painting to dry (iron, if necessary, when dry).

7. *Blot painting*

      a.   Fold paper in half.

      b.   Apply (or pour) paint (or ink) into middle of crease, or on one side.

      c.   Press sides together and rub with palm.

      d.   Open and let dry.

8. *Pointillist painting*

      a.   Prepare cotton balls, muslin, etc.

      b.   Place paint in shallow saucers.

  c. Dab piece of cotton in paint, one piece per color, and apply to paper in random fashion.

  d. Dry and display.

 9. *String painting*

  a. Drop one end of cord or string into paint.

  b. Pull out string and squeeze between fingers.

  c. Draw, drag string across paper.

  d. Dry and display.

10. *Spatter painting*

  a. Fill spray gun with paint.

  b. Arrange various objects (leaves, scissors, stencils) on paper and pin if necessary.

  c. Spray paper and objects with paint (or brush paint through a screen with toothbrush).

11. *Dry-brush stenciling*

  a. Prepare as with chalk, or paint stenciling.

  b. Dip brush in paint; remove most of paint on newspaper.

  c. Sweep brush from edge of stencil onto paper.

  d. Repeat with different colors and different position of stencil.

  e. Remove items from paper.

  f. Dry and display.

12. *Printing*

  a. Prepare sponges (various sizes, cut), vegetables (cross sections of carrots, potatoes, etc.), and fruits (orange, grapefruit sections).

  b. Soak stamp pad, or paper/cloth towels in paint(s), one pad for each color.

  c. Press finger tips, or vegetable, sponge, etc., on stamp.

  d. Apply object paint-side down to paper (repeat with various colors).

  e. Dry and display.

13. *Sundry techniques—with plastic squeeze bottles, straws, or rollers, apply paint to paper in various ways.*

SCULPTURE

Modeling and making stabiles and mobiles offer children their first exposure to three-dimensional art. As in finger painting, they come into direct contact with their material: squeezing, twisting, bending, rolling, pulling.

The younger children will work almost exclusively with clay and substitutes for clay. Three-year-olds usually lack the skill to handle stabiles or mobiles. Fours can make simple stabiles and mobiles. Fives can make relatively sophisticated mobiles and other constructions.

1. Modeling materials—for preparation and storage

Natural clay	Plasticine
Clay/dough	Modeling clay
Powder clay	Kiln
Wet clay	

2. Construction materials (accessories)

Pipe cleaners	Clothes hangers
Straws	Boxes
Shells	Tin foil
Wire (copper/brass—16–24 gauge)	Toothpicks
	Paper/string
Electrician's wire	Cardboard
Yarn	Styrofoam
Buttons/beads	Corks
Dowels	Tongue depressors
Ice cream sticks	Washers

3. Equipment

Firm table—with plastic or enamel top, or oilskin attached for modeling	Boards—for modeling
	Containers for clay—airtight

ACTIVITIES

1. Modeling
   a.   Prepare clay, and place on board or table (no newspapers—absorb too much moisture).
   b.   Keep water handy to keep clay moist and pliable.

    c. Free experimentation and manipulation with clay—realistic or unrealistic objects. Add accessories as desired.

    d. Allow object to dry—1 to 2 weeks; plasticine will never entirely dry or harden, nor will dough.

    e. Paint or fire, and display.

2. *Construction—stabiles*

    a. Prepare proper base—Styrofoam, clay, cork, etc.

    b. Use wire and pipe cleaners to form frame.

    c. Add other accessories as needed.

    d. (Variation: Make entire stabile out of different size boxes—paint, etc.)

3. *Construction—mobiles*

    a. Prepare objects—birds (paper), tin foil, light ready-made toys, etc.

    b. Attach fine string to each.

    c. Attach string to wire hanger.

    d. Balance objects on wire and hanger.

COLLAGES

Collages are two-dimensional constructions made by pasting instead of painting. Anything that can be pasted is material for a collage: papers, cloth, leaves, grass, reasonable flat or light objects of all kinds, colors and textures.

Start simply: give each child a scissors and a paste pot and only one kind of collage material (for example, colored construction paper cut into abstract shapes). It is a good idea to prepare only abstract shapes at any time, so that they can be anything the children imagine them to be.

After that, leave things up to the imagination—yours and theirs.

MATERIALS

    1. Design materials

Fabrics (solids, patterns)	Rough (tweed)
Smooth (polished cotton)	Soft (velvet)
Raised (corduroy)	Scratchy (burlap)

Papers	Greeting cards
Doilies	Excelsior
Construction	Aluminum foil
Gift wrapping	Straws
Newspapers	Wallpaper
Origami	Photographic paper
Cellophane	Corrugated cardboard
Miscellaneous	Buttons/beads
Fur feathers	Toothpicks
Absorbent cotton	Yarn/string
Rug scraps	Macaroni products
Linoleum scraps	Dry cereal
Oilcloth	Shells
Rug underlay	Gravel and sand
Sequins	Leather
Ribbon	Wood shavings
Cork	Eggshells

2. Equipment

Background material—construction paper, cardboard, wood
White, all-purpose glue
Home-made paste
Scissors—dull tips, sharp edges

ACTIVITIES

1. Prepare surface—cardboard, paper, wood.
2. Cut paper, cloth, etc., and otherwise prepare objcets to be used, various sizes and shapes (some of these may be prepared by instructor in advance).
3. Attach glue or paste to back side of each object, and arrange and affix to paper.
4. Allow to dry; hang and display.

HOME-MADE MATERIALS

The bibliography has a number of reference sources that teachers could use to help children prepare home-made materials. Some of the most popular are listed below.

HOME-MADE PAINTS

FINGER PAINT

(1) ½ box laundry starch (1½ cups)   1½ cups soap flakes
    1 quart boiling water   ½ cup talcum (optional)
Mix starch with enough cold water to make a paste; add boiling water stirring until clear and glossy. Add talcum. Cool mixture; add soap flakes, stirring until evenly distributed. Mixture should be thick. Pour into jars and cover. Keep in a cool place.

(2) Add in order given:
2 tablespoons glass starch and small amount of water to firm a paste.
1 cup boiling water; cook until clear; remove from fire.
½ cup granulated soap (not flakes); beat until smooth.

(3) 3 parts water   Glycerine
    1 part cornstarch   Food coloring
Bring water to a boil; dissolve starch and stir two together. Let mixture cool again. Store in a cool place.

(4) Mix 1 cup soap flakes, 1 cup cold water. Stir these ingredients into 7 cups of boiling water. Cook until thick (about five minutes). Cool in covered dish. Store in covered jar in a cool place.

(5) 12-ounce box cold-water starch   2 cups cold water
    Equal quantity of soap flakes   Powder paint for coloring
Mix together starch and soap flakes. Slowly add the water while stirring. Mix and beat until it reaches the consistency of whipped potatoes. Add powder or tempera paint to get desired color, keeping in mind that dark colors show up more effectively than light in final paintings. This recipe will make about 1½ pints, sufficient for an average-size class.

PAINT

    Soap flakes   Hand lotion
    Toothpaste   Food coloring
    Water

Mix soap flakes and water into smooth paste. Add a few drops of food coloring. Or, combine food coloring with hand lotion or toothpaste.

CLAY—HOME-MADE DOUGH/PASTE

CLAY

Well-prepared clay is soft and moist (consistency of bread dough) and will not stick to hands.

(1) *NATURAL CLAY (decomposed rock with many impurities in it)*

Test soil for clay by taking handful and squeezing it—if it holds, clay will retain its shape.

Method of preparation: Place clay soil in pail half filled with water; strain mixture into another pail. Strain again and again through double thickness of cheesecloth, taking care not to pour sediments through it. Let stand until settled; pour off water. Let clay dry from twelve to twenty-four hours and then make into balls.

(2) *POWDER CLAY (or clay dust)*

Commercially marketed and available in brick form or in bag or box. Inexpensive. Sold at art-supply stores, potteries, or play-equipment companies.

Method of preparation: Pound clay into fine powder (from brick form) and mix 2½ parts of clay to 1 part water. Mix well in advance of time of use. Blending of clay and water can be achieved best by placing powder in cloth bag, tying top of bag, and soaking in water overnight. Knead thoroughly to remove air bubbles and excess water. Slamming or pounding the clay on a flat surface will help.

(3) *WET CLAY*

Available commercially in brick form; already mixed and ready for use. Most convenient way of securing clay but the most expensive. Secured through art-supply house, school-supply houses, department stores, or potteries.

All of these clays should be wrapped in a damp cloth, placed in plastic bags, or kept in a well-ventilated crock or zink-lined box. Any clay, after use, or if not used over a period of time, needs water and kneading to be brought back to prime condition.

DOUGH ("homemade clay")

This clay does not harden thoroughly, but by increasing proportion of salt, a hard crust will form overnight.

The advantages of this material lies in the speed of preparation, the children's active independent preparation, opportunities for coloring it (from salt shakers filled with powdered tempera paint or drops of vegetable coloring), and by its readily manipulative qualities. It can be eaten safely, but initial taste is usually enough to satisfy curiosity.

Dough can be baked, but the shapes tend to swell and chip easily. If the shapes are to be used as hanging decorations, holes for threading should be punched before they are left to dry or put to bake.

1 cup salt
2½ cups flour
1 cup water
¼ teaspoon cooking oil
¼ to ½ teaspoon food coloring (if color is desired)

Mix thoroughly. Place in a covered plastic bowl overnight (twelve to fifteen hours).

Before using, add a little more flour (if necessary) for desired consistency.

PASTE

(1) *PASTE (homemade—1)*

1 cup flour	1 cup cold water
2¼ cups boiling water	1 teaspoon powdered alum
¾ teaspoon oil of wintergreen	
¾ teaspoon oil of wintergreen	

Mix flour with cold water; stir until smooth. Add boiling water; stir. Cook in double boiler over low heat until smooth. Add alum; stir until smooth. Remove from fire; add oil of wintergreen when mixture is cooling. Store in covered jars in a cool place.

(2) *PASTE (for sawdust puppets)*

1 cup flour	6 teaspoons powdered glue
6 cups water	2 teaspoons oil of cloves
6 tablespoons powdered alum	

Blend together flour and water. Add alum, glue, and oil of cloves. Blend mixture well.

(3) *WHEAT PASTE (Warning: Some brands contain toxic ingredients—check label.)*

1½ cups boiling water	Add ½ tablespoon salt (for preser-
Add 2 teaspoons wheat flour;	vative)
stir well	

(4) *PASTE (homemade—2)*

1 Pound white dextrine mixed with enough water to make stiff paste. Heat in double boiler. Add 1 ounce salicylic acid and/or benzoate of soda. Cool and store in cool place in covered jars.

CHAPTER 3
MIXING ART AND SCIENCE

Cooking

Cooking, that mysterious blend of art and science that affects all our lives, is especially intriguing to preschool children. It enables them to participate in the process by which their mothers (and, much less frequently, their fathers) take certain raw materials and transform them into the meals that go inside their bodies.

Cooking is· intrinsically interesting to children. Beyond that, however, the preparation of food can be integrated into a preschool curriculum to provide children with a variety of opportunities for learning. It involves both quantitative and qualitative experiences: measuring, counting, and seeing things change as they are mixed, heated, and cooled. Finally, cooking is one of the relatively few educational activities in which evaluation follows almost immediately after performance: children don't have to wait while a teacher ''grades'' what they've done—they can taste it themselves and grade their own skill.

Cooking requires more ingenuity and adaptation on the part of preschool teachers than most other activities, since their range of possibilities in this area depends heavily on the equipment available to them. Ideally, teachers should have at their disposal both a refrigerator and a range, including an oven. Lacking all these items, however, the teacher can try to improvise: a simple hot plate or electric frying pan can enable the teacher and his or her class to prepare many drinks and simple recipes such as puddings and gelatin desserts, scrambled eggs, and French toast.

Some items—carrots, tomatoes, nuts, cheese spreads, melons, etc.—require no cooking at all but still make it possible for children to test the results of their own efforts, as well as to learn such subsidiary lessons as cooperation, estimating the quanti-

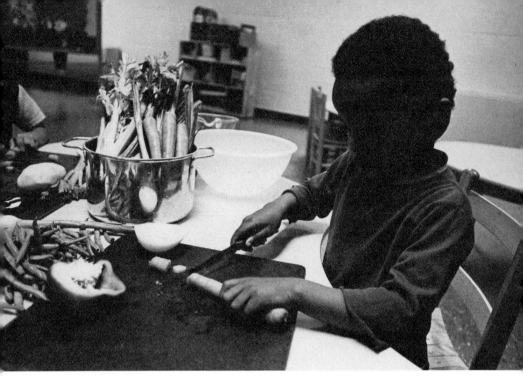

As in art, with cooking it's the process that matters to the child, and the end product is usually forgotten in a short time.

ties necessary to serve a number of children, and dividing food into portions.

The major value of cooking, then, lies more in the *process* than in the *product.* The purpose is not to feed children but to teach them— or stimulate them to learn for themselves—a variety of lessons that can be interestingly introduced through the preparation of food.

Among the most important of these lessons is conveying some sense of *nutrition*—basically, the idea that food varies in its value to humans and that different kinds of it are necessary for wholesome growth. Life isn't all spinach—nor is it all ice cream.

Here are a few simple criteria for choosing cooking experiments for the preschool:

1. It should be simple enough so that, while it demonstrates the benefits of preparing food, the preparation can be done successfully by the children.

2. The project needs to be completed within a relatively brief (an hour or less to begin with) period of time. Remember that children have short attention spans, and most enjoy activities whose results are apparent quickly. If they have to wait for a couple of hours before their "creation" is ready, children are likely to lose interest in it and to forget that their own efforts produced it.

3. The project should be related to their tastes and age levels. While they may find all the preparation necessary for crepe suzettes tedious and unrewarding, they will all understand simple pancakes.

4. Relate the procedures involved in a certain recipe to other areas of the curriculum—to counting, for example, or demonstrating changes in certain materials under conditions of heat, cold, or mixing.

5. The project should be handled without elaborate precautions for safety.

In short, while trying to make the project interesting for the children, make it easy on yourself. Start with something simple: a salad, a powdered soft drink mix such as Kool-Aid, or an easy gelatin dessert such as Jell-O. Let the children help with each step. As they become more experienced and proficient in their handling of quantities of food and with kitchen equipment introduce more complex recipes.

At some point, involve the children from beginning to end: write down the ingredients for a recipe; conduct a "field trip" to a local store to buy the ingredients; bring the children back and begin the necessary measuring and preparation. (Check ahead of time with the manager for the store's least busy hour, so that the children can explore the shelves without interfering—and maybe even get an impromptu lecture from the butcher, produce manager, or cashier.)

Cooking requires more careful planning and supervision than most preschool activities, especially since it entails the use of heat and because the results will be judged more strictly by the children themselves. Try recipes beforehand, so that you will know exactly the steps and motions involved and will be able to judge the best ways to allow participation by the children.

COOKING ACTIVITIES

You can develop a repertoire of simple recipes simply by leafing

through cookbooks. Look not only for those that require a minimum of preparation—the use of heat, etc.—but also for those that utilize natural foods (carrots, apples, melons, pineapple, celery) that can be combined on platters or in salads for eye appeal. Don't overlook the use of spices such as cinnamon or salt, or sweeteners such as honey, brown sugar, or regular sugar, which alter the taste of simple foods such as bread and butter or raw vegetables and fruits—thus giving the children some sense of accomplishment without elaborate preparation.

Here are some "finger foods" that require nothing more than cutting or tearing—plus counting:

Apple wedges	Banana thirds
Carrot sticks	Celery, cabbage leaves
Celery sticks	Orange wedges
Spinach leaves	Parsley pieces
Cucumber sticks	Tomato wedges
Turnip sticks	Watercress
Tangerine pieces	Plum pieces
Raw potato pieces	Pear sections
Cabbage leaves	Green-pepper pieces
Endive pieces	Melon wedges
Fresh pineapple pieces	Whole strawberries
Seedless grapes	Fresh peach wedges
Fresh apricot halves	Whole radishes

MAIN DISHES

1. CREAM SOUP

> 3 cups vegetable puree   3 cups milk
> Salt to taste

Combine vegetable puree with milk. Heat. Season to taste.

2. MEAT BALLS

> 1 pound ground lean beef   ¾ cup soft bread crumbs
> 2 teaspoons salt   1 slightly beaten egg

Mix all ingredients and shape into balls. Place into well-greased baking pan. Bake in a moderate oven twenty to thirty minutes.

With adequate attention to safety, preschoolers can be allowed to use knives, ranges, electric fry pans, and ovens.

3. SALMON LOAF

1 pound canned salmon	1 slightly beaten egg
1½ cups soft bread crumbs	1 cup milk
1 teaspoon lemon juice	

Drain liquid from salmon. Combine all ingredients. Shape into a loaf in a greased pan. Bake in a moderate oven (375°) twenty-five to thirty minutes.

4. SCRAMBLED EGGS

4 eggs	2 teaspoons butter
¼ cup milk or cream	¼ teaspoon salt

Simple foods such as fruits, vegetables, and drinks can be gotten together fastest, and that helps speed things along to the "sense of accomplishment" stage.

Beat eggs slightly, add liquid and salt. Heat butter in top of double boiler. Pour eggs into melted butter. Stir with fork until creamy — about 3 minutes.

DESSERTS

1. PLAIN CAKE

2 cups sifted cake flour	½ cups sugar
2½ teaspoons double action baking powder	1 teaspoon vanilla flavoring
½ cup vegetable shortening	
1 teaspoon salt	

Sift dry ingredients (baking powder, flour, sugar, salt) into large mixing bowl. Drop in shortening. Mix milk and vanilla. Add to other ingredients. Beat two minutes by clock (150 strokes per minute). If using mixer, beat on slow to medium speed. Add unbeaten eggs. Beat two minutes longer. Scrape bowl and spoon frequently. Pour into two greased 8- or 9-inch layer pans or a large square pan. Bake in a moderate oven (375°) about twenty-five minutes.

2. ROLLED COOKIES

3½ cups sifted flour	1½ cups sugar
1 teaspoon baking powder	2 well-beaten eggs
½ teaspoon salt	1½ teaspoons vanilla flavoring
1 cup shortening	

Sift baking powder, salt and flour. Cream shortening, add sugar and continue to beat until light. Add well beaten eggs and vanilla. Combine dry ingredients and cream mixture. Mix all thoroughly and chill. Roll on lightly floured board and cut with cookie cutter, or form small balls of the dough and flatten with bottom of glass tumbler or with palm of hand or with tines of fork. Bake in a hot oven (400°) six to ten minutes. Makes about six dozen cookies

3. GINGER BREAD

1 egg	½ cup molasses
½ cup sugar	½ cup hot water
¼ cup butter	2 cups sifted flour
1 teaspoon cinnamon	1 teaspoon soda
1 teaspoon ginger	1 teaspoon salt

Beat egg, sugar, and molasses together until light. Melt butter in hot water and add slowly to egg mixture. Sift dry ingredients (soda, salt, spices, and flour). Add to wet ingredients. Beat well. Pour into greased 8-inch pan. Bake in a moderate oven (350°) for about twenty minutes.

As a kind of graduation ceremony for your cooking class, consider holding a breakfast for parents, prepared entirely by the children. After a few weeks or months of practice, the children should be able to handle scrambled eggs or pancakes. An after-breakfast discussion by the preschool teacher or director might point out that breakfast is not just an aimless "busy work" activity for the children, but one that taught them a number of skills in the process.

Boys as well as girls enjoy participating in cooking activities. However, once in awhile a few boys may resist cooking because, in their own homes, they see that this one sphere of human activity is mainly reserved for females. Don't try to talk boys into participating if they express the sentiment that cooking is "only for girls." Instead, develop the groundwork for an interesting class discussion by having all the children ask their mothers and fathers why women usually do the cooking. Many a father buried behind an evening newspaper will emerge to respond interestingly to the question, Who are better cooks, men or women? by citing the "fact" that most leading restaurants employ men as chefs.

The class might offer its own answer to the men-women question in competition between boys and girls. Competition between individuals can be damaging to preschool children, but competition between groups—so that individual performances are not thrown into embarrassing relief—can stimulate harder work and a sense of solidarity in cooperation: whose pancakes, cupcakes, sandwiches taste better? If women do most of the cooking, *why* do they do it? Have the children take an inventory of the cookbooks at home: Are the authors men or women?

Again, cooking in the preschool is not an end in itself but an opportunity to interest children in a variety of unfamiliar concepts—quantity, chemical change, nutrition—through a familiar vehicle. To repeat Piaget, "The half-familiar teaches"; the preschool teacher's job is to find bridges between what the child knows and what is worth learning. Cooking is one such bridge.

Woodworking

Like cooking, woodworking requires close supervision. For that reason—again, like cooking—it is often not included in many preschool programs. Yet few activities appeal more to children, or offer them a chance to do and learn so much.

Beyond the sheer pleasure of banging and sawing, woodworking calls into play a range of physical and mental skills: small and large-muscle skills; visual skills; and the ability to invent, imagine, plan, follow a sequence toward a goal, and the like.

Some children may have had some experience with woodworking at home; otherwise, introduce them to it only after they have had experience with blocks and other construction material. One way to begin is to let them make things with bits and pieces of wood used as blocks. Once they've made something, help them glue it together. When they seem to have had enough experience in working with different sizes and shapes of wood, introduce them to the simplest sort of woodworking. Children should be permitted to create their own pieces of work.

In the beginning, the children will need a good deal of help in using equipment. Start them off with basic tools such as the saw and hammer. When they have mastered these, they can go on to more difficult tools such as the plane and the drill.

EQUIPMENT

1. Workbenches (23 to 25 inches high, 30- to 40-inch top)
2. Set of uniform boxes
3. Storage box for wood
4. Pegboard for keeping tools

A hammer, a nail, some wood—what child could resist the offer to work with these? And what teacher could resist the chance to let the preschooler develop muscle and visual skills while creating something new and special?

MATERIALS

NOTE: Obtain standard tools, not children's play tools. There are standard tools available in smaller sizes.

1. TOOLS

Claw hammer—7 to 13
   ounce, broad head, well
   balanced (sharp angle on
   claw)
Crosscut saw (12 to 24, 8
   to 10 point, for cutting
   across grain)
Pliers (optional)

Screwdrivers—different sizes
(optional)
Block plane
Try square
Half-round file (6 inch)
Vise (jam not less than 2½
inch)
Iron clamps (optional)
C clamp—5- to 6-inch
opening
Sandpaper—no. 1½
Miter box (Stanley 116)
Drill
Nails (pound boxes—4 to 5
penny boxes, 8 penny
finish, 8 penny common,
10 penny common, thin
wire nails and brads ¾
inch and 1 inch, 16 or 17
gauge)
12-inch rule
Screws (optional)
Brace and bits (#4, #8,
#12, #16—optional)
Carpenter's pencils (optional)
Glue
Paint (poster)

2. *WOOD*

Soft pine (yellow or white), poplar (no. 2 and no. 3
common)
Suggested sizes:
1, 2, 4, 6, 10 × ½ × 36 inches
1, 2, 4, 6 × 1 × 36 inches
2 × 2 × 36 inches
Dowels—varying diameter or length

ACTIVITIES

1. *USE OF TOOLS*

   a. HAMMER

   Keep hand at end of handle.
   Fit hammer (striking surface) to nail (head).
   Start with light tapping.
   Hit nail firmly (only part-way until square).
   Always nail thinner piece to thicker piece.

   b. SAWING

   (1) Cross-cut

   Mark wood where cut is to be made.
   Set wood with clamps, vise and miter box.
   Keep working point as close as possible jams.
   Stand directly in front of wood.
   Hold blade at 40 to 50° angle.
   Downstroke—take bite (apply pressure—two
      hands if necessary).
   Upstroke—no bite (rest).

   (2) Coping saw (sometimes difficult for young
      children)

   Mark wood where cut is to be made.
   Set vise, clamps, etc.
   Pull saw *straight up and down.*
   Change position of blade before attempting to make
      an extreme curved or angle cut.

   c. SANDING

   Attach sandpaper to block of wood.
   Use coarse and fine grades as needed.
   Always sand with grain, never across or diagonally.
   Always sand elements before joining or nailings.

NOTE: The use of the screwdriver, plane, pliers, and the large drill is difficult for young children and probably not to be undertaken. The combined motion of grasping, pushing, squeezing, twisting, and pulling requires a high degree of coordination. To the extent these tools are required in a woodworking project, the instructor should probably do it her/himself.

2. *SUGGESTED PROJECTS*

Creative work by children
Pull toys—truck, train, ship,
    airplane, boats, with
    dowels, spools, wheels,
    string
Traffic signs
Bird feeders
Cork villages

Puzzles
Simple animals and cars
Animal bed
Hobby horse
Human figures (wood base +
    + pipe cleaners + spools
    + clothesline)

Language

While it pervades the preschool environment as thoroughly as the air the children breathe, language is sometimes an activity in itself, especially when stories are read or told. Most preschool language experiences, however, occur naturally, in the course of other activities—as the children talk, explain, listen, and look at books. Many activities not specifically termed "language" involve skills that will later help the child in reading and writing: when he works with puzzles or hammers nails into wood, he is sharpening the eye-hand coordination he will need for writing; when he distinguishes between colors, or sizes and shapes of blocks, he is developing the kind of visual discrimination that he will need for reading.

Unless a teacher knows what he or she is doing and has been trained, odds are overwhelming that more harm than good will be done by trying to introduce children directly into reading and writing. The entire subject of early reading and "reading readiness" is a matter of considerable dispute among experts. The fact is that we still do not really know what determines reading readiness in a child, let alone when any given child is ready. We do know that some children seem ready early and some late. Even assuming that we could determine the right moment for introducing every child to reading, we have not yet come up with a reading method that works equally well with every child. Nothing is worse than to push a child when he or she is not ready, or to make him or her anxious or nervous about progress or lack of progress toward reading. With reading as with every other developmental skill, the job of the preschool teacher is to provide stimuli for reading in an atmosphere that encourages without compelling, and to remain alert for signs in individual children that indicate their readiness to embark on their personal exploration of symbolic meaning. While helping those children who do display a curiosity about printed words, the teacher should not display so much pleasure in their interest that other children feel deficient unless they, too, show the same interest.

Thus this chapter is not concerned with reading and writing as such but with methods that will help the teacher provide stimuli for those skills—opportunities for children to demonstrate that they have attained the "moment of readiness."

By the time children reach the preschool age, they have not only learned how to talk but have done a great deal of it. Even among children of the same age, however, there are striking differences in one or more aspects of verbal development—in coherence, articulation, vocabulary, and the like. Varying maturational levels and home environments account for these differences. Language development of the child from a "disadvantaged" home environment differs not simply in degree but in kind from that of a child from a more "advantaged" environment.

Children originally learn to talk by listening and imitating. Listening and imitating continue to play a large role in their language development in preschool. The teacher who talks to children clearly and carefully (but at the same time easily and naturally), and gives them full and undivided attention when they are talking, is encouraging the children to talk and listen that way. It is principally and powerfully by example that the teacher "teaches" children to talk fully and fluently, and to listen attentively. There is no better way to destroy a child's confidence than by constantly correcting his speech while he is talking—or to discourage his spontaneous, pleasurable growth in the proper use of language than by insisting on stilted, textbook talk. The basic purpose of language is to express meaning; rules of grammar and syntax can come later. Language development at this point is a matter of encouraging children to match verbal symbols with their observations—not to discourage them by pointing out the inaccuracies in their attempts to do so. The Russian child cited by Chukovsky who described a bald man as "a man with a barefoot head'' said something cute; she also demonstrated a precocious ability to transfer concepts from one context to another, and a verbal ingenuity that many adults cannot match— perhaps because their imagination in using language has been subdued by too much stress on ''correctness.''

The focus, instead, ought to be upon expanding the child's experience of language as a living thing—as something that adds to his or her experience and powers, rather than as something that makes everything dead and lifeless. Sylvia Ashton-Warner's book *Teacher* (1963) and Kornei Chukovsky's book *From Two to Five* (1968) suggest ways of bringing language to life in early childhood learning.

BOOKS

Although their attitudes depend largely on how much their parents read, and read to them, children generally come to school with a fairly well-formed sense of the importance of the printed word. They may know about newspapers and about signs that say stop or go; they may have received letters or cards, and have drawn pictures on a letter mother is sending to grandma.

In the preschool classroom this sense is reinforced in a variety of ways. Children see the teacher writing on the blackboard; their names printed over the hooks where their coats are hung; the word *block* along with the picture of a block on the block shelf. They listen as the teacher reads them a story from a book illustrated with bright pictures. They know that the pictures show what the words say.

Sometimes a child takes a book off the display shelf and looks through it, turns the pages the way the teacher does, and maybe even pretends to read (if it is a story that has been read to him several times before) by reciting the story to himself in conjunction with the pictures. Often the teacher reads or tells stories the child can act out—with his fingers or his whole body. Sometimes when a child plays, at home or in school, he or she imagines being one of the people in one of the places in one of the stories the teacher read in school.

SELECTION AND USE OF BOOKS

Buying books blindly—even on the recommendation of respected authorities—is the worst way to select books for the preschool. Since you and your children are going to have to live with these books, only you can decide which books are best for you.

From Nancy Larrick's book entitled *A Parent's Guide to Children's Reading* (1969), and other appropriate, more recent lists of publications, work up a basic list of books that seem worth inspecting. Then browse through your local library, bookstore, or even other preschools, and add to and subtract from your list.

Your selections should be very broad in content and format. Some books, especially those for the younger children, will be primarily picture books with little text. Some will have more text. Some will have nursery rhymes, "real life" stories, information about the natural or man-made world, imaginative stories. They should be as sturdy as possible (hard-cover library editions, if you can afford them). The illustrations should be colorful and, where essential for understanding, simple and clear. The narrative or story line ought to be simple enough so that children can follow it without confusion; there should not be so many characters that children cannot keep track of them.

In regard to reading itself, experts disagree on the inclusion of fairy tales and fantasy in the preschool literary repertoire. Some feel that children should not be exposed to fantasy until they are around seven or eight years old, when there is little danger of their confusing it with reality. Others believe that fantasy is not only healthy but downright desirable, enabling children to control with their imaginations a world so beyond their understanding.

Surely, the cruel, the frightening, and the violent should be avoided—though anybody disturbed by the violence in children's TV cartoons ought to reread Grimm's fairy tales. And fantasy

Preschoolers will frequently go through a book that has been read to them many times before and recite the story while looking at the pictures and turning the pages.

should be presented precisely as fantasy—as make-believe, as pretense.

Once these cautions are observed, there seems to be no reason to think that fantasy in stories (for example, "Wynken, Blynken and Nod" and "The Owl and the Pussycat") is harmful—any more than the fantasy that children normally employ in their play. Chukovsky argues that children have little difficulty distinguishing between fact and fantasy and that it is, in fact, precisely because they know something *cannot* exist or happen in the real world that they delight in their ability to *make* it happen in their minds. The ability to develop fantasies is probably not far removed from the ambitious dreams entertained by adults that lead them to make plans for a better future. In any case, it is likely that the saccharine, stereotyped children's books that present a totally optimistic, sunny view of reality are more damaging—both to the mind and to a child's interest in reading— than the clever fictions of the best fairy tales. Imagination has powered most of mankind's greatest achievements, and the ability to make imaginative use of information—to ask, "What if...?"—is an important component of intellectual developments.

The books selected for the preschool should be attractively displayed on a low shelf, or rack, or table, so that children can easily handle and look at them during the day. Sometimes the teacher should let a child take a favorite book home, or bring to school a book he has at home.

READING TO CHILDREN

Children are, by nature, active and energetic young beings. But there are times—especially in the afternoon of an all-day session—when they need some rest and relaxation. These seem to be the best times for reading to them or telling them stories.

As a check on his or her own observations, the teacher should invite the children to decide which story they want to hear. Often something that has happened or is going to happen—like a planned trip, or some activity the children have recently engaged in—will suggest a book or story.

Gather in a quiet corner, relatively free of bright decorations or materials that might distract the children. Sit on a low chair or on the floor (not in a high chair or behind a desk) with the children comfortably sitting near you. As you read, try to hold the pages of the book toward the children, so that they can follow the illustrations as you read.

For both teacher and children, reading should be an active experience. Read in a natural voice but with genuine interest and animation—as if relating a personal experience. Without overdoing it, try different voices for different characters. As much as possible, look directly at the children as you read—as if, again, telling them a personal story.

Even when resting, children are naturally restless, and they should be allowed to move and wriggle and grimace while being read to. If they seem unduly restless, the teacher may have chosen the wrong time for reading. Children should be encouraged to ask questions during the story, but be careful not to let a question become a digression or an interruption. There are a number of ways to stimulate the involvement and imagination of children: by hesitating, for example, before the last word of a recurrent phrase so that the children can supply the word or, in the context of what happens next, by asking, ''And what do you think the fireman did next?'' ''What flew overhead?'' ''How do you know?'' or by having the children use their imagination by asking them, ''What do you think is in the big box?''

Sometimes (not too often, or the break becomes irritating), when the teacher reads a word that he or she thinks some children might not know (*crown* in ''Jack and Jill''; *porridge* in the ''Three Bears''; or an abstract word like *enthusiasm),* he or she might ask ''Does anybody know what 'crown' means?'' If no one does, the word can be explained briefly (with care taken not to dwell on it and break the continuity of the story). By doing this, the children are encouraged to become aware of individual words and their meanings and to ask what a word means when they do not understand it.

POEMS, RHYMES, FINGER PLAYS

Children respond well to the ''action aspects''—the rythms, the sounds, the word play—of poems and rhymes. For this reason these are best used not at set times but more or less

With the use of reading tapes, children can "read" a book on their own any time they want.

spontaneously—when everybody seems in the mood—or in relation to some specific event or activity.

Memorize a number of finger plays—short verses, rhymes, and the like that children can act out with their fingers. When introducing one for the first time, go through it once yourself and then have the children do each verse after you. The bibliography at the end of the book contains several finger-play collections.

LISTENING POSTS, TAPES, RECORDS

Many technical tools are now available to permit youngsters to develop and pursue their own language interests. A wide variety of tapes and records should be available to children. Further, children should be taught to handle the equipment on their own to help build, among other things, a feeling of independence.

GETTING CHILDREN TO TALK

Though a good deal of conversation goes on during the school day, few occasions arise which call for children to talk at length and by themselves to the rest of the group—to relate an experience, to tell a story, to explain how something works. Unless the teacher deliberately sets up such situations, then, the children have little opportunity to develop their ability to handle more complex kinds of speech, to organize and express their thoughts with some sense of sequence and coherence.

The teacher should encourage this kind of speech without becoming too rigid or artificial. One time-honored technique is ''show and tell''—an activity in which each child brings an object to school and tells the class about it. More recently, this activity has been increasingly rejected as simply too formal and demanding for children who have yet to overcome their shyness before groups. The same objective can be accomplished by encouraging children to talk in pairs on play telephones before the class, or to dictate a story, experience, letter, or rhyme.

Dictation can be done with a single child or with a group. Children can, for example, take turns in suggesting lines for a poem or a story to be composed by a small group or the entire class. Occasions and opportunities that lend themselves to dictation will arise during the ordinary course of events. When one child is sick, for example, the children might want to dictate a letter to him. Once children get the idea that although they cannot write, the teacher (or tape recorder) can write for them, they will initiate occasions for dictating. You may want on occasion to experiment with a tape recorder; after overcoming their initial wariness toward the recorder, many children enjoy their ability to make a machine talk back to them, as well as the strange sound of their own voices.

There is no necessity to go overboard on buying audio equipment; sturdy, easy-to-use cassette tape recorders (which require no threading from one spool to another) can be purchased for thirty dollars. Instead of one elaborate, high-fidelity outfit, get three or four utilitarian recorders, and let several groups record a play or ''discussion'' for later listening by the entire class.

Once in a while you might type out (on a typewriter with large type) a child's dictated story on separate pieces of paper. The child can then draw pictures to illustrate his or her story, and bind all the pages together in a book.

A good deal of talk can revolve around experiences shared by the class, especially around walking trips they may take into the woods or to some construction activity or a firehouse, and so on. After these trips, the children can sit down and discuss what they saw and heard, or perhaps talk about some leaves or stones or other items they may have gathered during the walk.

Since children cannot go everywhere and see everything, a variety of vicarious experiences can be brought to them by inviting people from various walks of life to come in and talk to them—describing, illustrating, and if possible demonstrating what they do. Mailman, fireman, policeman, milkman, lawyer, judge, forest ranger, businessman, jeweler, tailor, carpenter, poet, nurseryman, farmer, painter, airplane pilot, musician, sculptor, actor, photographer, elected official, dancer, biologist, architect, bricklayer, plumber, doctor, tree surgeon, sailor—the possibilities are numerous.

WORD GAMES

The child gets a good deal of sheer physical fun out of playing games with words and with the sounds of words. Giving the child as many opportunities as possible to have fun with words is probably the best way of interesting him or her in language.

Here are two word games:

1. Ask children to complete similes: "As large as a ...," "As green as a...." This is best done spontaneously, when the children are looking at something green or large.

2. Ask children to give you rhymes for words you say: dog, fog, log; cat, fat, rat. Or, for variation, give them couplets with one rhyme missing: "I'm thinking of a word that sounds like tree, I buzz and I sting, so I'm a ...."

Once you get into these, variations will undoubtedly suggest themselves.

LISTENING

The ability to listen attentively and to discriminate between sounds is an important and often overlooked language skill.

Here are some games that children enjoy and that require active, attentive listening:

1. Ask the children to close their eyes and not make a sound. Go to a far corner of the room, and as softly as possible say a child's name. Each child, as he hears his name called, opens his eyes, gets up, and as quietly as he can walks to that corner of the room.

2. Ask the children (again silent, with eyes closed) to identify various sounds: clap hands, ring a bell, blow bubbles in water, tap wood or the rim of a glass, stamp feet.

3. Ask children (again silent, with eyes closed) to identify animal sounds you make.

4. Ask children (again silent, with eyes closed) to repeat a sentence you say as softly as you can. If children do not at first "get" it, wait for utter silence and then try again. If they still cannot make it out, say it again but slightly louder—and so on.

Physical devices – and lots of them, such as flash cards, labels on toys, and snapshots with words – all help the preschooler to develop word-object relations.

READING AND WRITING READINESS

Many, if not all, of the above activities could be classified under the umbrella of "readiness." Most children of preschool age are far from ready to enter a formal reading and writing program but are in a position to enjoy a variety of experiences that emphasize the use and importance of letters and labels/signs and symbols.

The best place to start is with each child's name: print it in large letters on his locker or storage box, or over his coat hook. Tie it in with a picture or a drawing, made by the child or by one of his classmates. If you have a Polaroid camera, you might want to use a snapshot of each child as the picture.

You might later use snapshots and names in various sorts of matching games. For example, mix up the names and snapshots and let the children try to match them properly. Or let them try to group the snapshots and names in alphabetical order.

In general, look for opportunities to print a child's name to identify something that is his—not only his possessions but also a painting, for example, in which he takes some pride.

Beyond this, use names and pictures together to identify things and places in the room: the word *cup,* for example, with a picture of a cup on the cup shelf. Encourage the use of signs in the children's play: stop and go signs, for example, when they are playing with cars and trucks.

Have plenty of alphabet letters available—made out of wood or other durable material and covered with sandpaper or a rough cloth. The children can feel the letters, trace them (you might need to show them how to trace them), and arrange them. In addition, there are simple readiness materials available that will assist children in developing visual skills (left-right orientation), memory skills, and symbolic or structural skills relating to letters and numbers.

CHAPTER 6
WHAT CAN THEY COUNT ON?

Numbers

To many present and former students, mathematics is the most mystifying of all school subjects. Most of us acquire the rudiments of arithmetic necessary for success in school and for everyday use in life: addition, subtraction, division, multiplication; any form of higher mathematics survives in our memories simply as a puzzling phase of education with little bearing on our careers.

In *Arithmetic and Mathematics* (1968), Carl Bereiter says that the majority of schoolchildren "drop out" of math—intellectually if not physically—at either fractions or algebra. The basic reason, he believes, is that mathematics is presented to most students simply as a series of operations to be performed, not as a process to be understood.

The same observation might be made of many other subjects in the school curriculum: history presented as a series of dates to be memorized rather than as the analysis of cause and effect in social change; literature presented as a list of books and poems that are "required" reading for every educated person rather than as an abundance of personal expressions of the human experience from which a student may select a comparative few that give him pleasure; physics and chemistry presented as charts of atomic weights and prefabricated laboratory experiments rather than as an explication of methods by which man has explored the questions that his physical world presents to him.

The emphasis in preschool, as in the upper grades, should be on conveying to the child an understanding of what numbers are *for,* why they are needed, and their occurrence in everyday life, rather than as objects in themselves. The high school and college student, if he is lucky in his mathematics teachers, may develop an interest in numbers as abstract entities, totally divorced

from things to be measured, counted, weighed, timed, or otherwise quantified. The preschool student, however, is too young for such purely intellectual pleasures. Rather than regarding numbers as an activity in itself, therefore, the teacher should look for opportunities to call attention to numbers as aspects of other activities.

The child does in fact encounter numbers in many forms in the preschool: in books (sequence of pages), in storing blocks (size and shape), in woodwork (size, shape, dimension), in water play (volume), and so on. The day's activities present many natural opportunities for the use of numbers—in distributing the right number of crayons and pieces of paper, for example, counting out sandwiches or cups, or getting the right number of coat hangers. The teacher's job is to make children aware of their encounters with numbers in an unobstrusive way so that they learn various methods of quantification naturally and so that their various experiences with numbers amplify and reinforce each other.

Counting is the most basic and most obvious number activity, but by no means the only one. Numbering is essentially a way to quantify objects or experiences and as such has several dimensions, each of which can suggest activities such as weighing, telling time, and counting.

WEIGHING

One simple preschool toy consists of a balance and a set of plastic numbers—the two weighing twice as much as the one, the four twice as much as the two, and so forth. By balancing a three and a two on one side of the balance and a five on the other, the child develops a sense of equal quantity as well as of addition and subtraction.

Similarly, the teacher can devise a simple scale for weighing or balancing other items—three little cookies against two big

Numbers in the abstract sense don't make much of an impression on any of us, let alone preschoolers. But one five-cent piece plus another five-cent piece adds up to one ten-cent piece. And that's a dime, and it goes in this cash register, right?

ones, for example—and can bring an ordinary bathroom scale into class so that the children can weigh themselves. The idea of number can be built in as a way for the children to *find out* about the world and themselves; have them guess beforehand which of three youngsters weighs the most, which the least (taking care, of course, not to embarrass anyone), and then have them check the accuracy of their estimates with the scale.

TELLING TIME

Clocks are excellent ways of introducing children to numbers and their function in measuring the duration of activities. The teacher need not set out formally to teach children to tell time; rather, it can be approached informally, by having the children note the position of the hands on the clock at significant moments of the day—such as lunch or snack time and the time for leaving school. Try in all number activities to relate the numbers to things and activities that are important to the children, so that they understand number as a part of their *own* lives rather than as a separate entity.

COUNTING

Start with the child: How many fingers and toes does he or she have? Two ears, two hands—what else are there two of? Branch out to other objects the child is interested in: beads, dolls, blocks, cars, the number of colors in his paint box, of people in his family. Soon the child will begin counting without reference to any specific object.

Any kind of measurement lends itself to number as well as introducing children to the tools of measurement: height, temperature, distance, thickness, area. The preschool should make available to children a variety of materials specifically designed to encourage different kinds of mathematical learning—such items as Cuisenaire rods, unit blocks, number and geometric puzzles, counting cards, dominoes, and so forth. In addition to these materials, many items commonly found around the home can be used: clocks, thermometers, playing cards, tape measures, rulers and yardsticks, measuring cups, and calendars.

Music and Movement

For the young child, music and movement go together. Music not only moves the child but seems to spring from movement itself; both seem to have their roots in rhythm—in the discernible pattern of rise and fall, of appearance and disappearance, that seems to underly virtually every kind of change (the seasons, youth and age, light and dark) in the world.

Like water play, music can both soothe the overactive and aggressive and stimulate the withdrawn and inhibited. It gives the one greater control and the other greater freedom, and it seems to afford every child a unique feeling of oneness with both himself and others.

It follows that music ought to be among the most enjoyable and open activities in the preschool. It ought especially to be one in which children can freely and spontaneously use their bodies, voices, and imaginations.

Unfortunately, music is often the most controlled and constricted activity; children are treated as if they were training to be a crack drill team or marching band. *This probably happens because most teachers are not musicians.* Unsure and unskilled, they are sometimes afraid that things will get out of hand if they do not apply a tight rein. And often, of course, they simply do not know what to do.

Most experts agree that the first thing to do is relax. The teacher does not have to be a skilled musician to play a guitar or piano, or dance well, or even be able to carry a tune. All the teacher needs, one authority has said, is "a good sense of humor; a healthy imagination; a willingness to crawl on all fours."

In addition, the nonmusical teacher (or the teacher who *thinks* he or she is nonmusical) should choose musical compositions

Striking-type instruments, such as triangles and drums, are easily controlled by a child and at the same time offer a creative outlet for individual interpretation.

for voice and rhythm that are simple, easy, and readily converted into games—such as finger plays and motion songs. The teacher should know a song well before teaching it, keep introductions short and simple (the fun is in doing it, not in listening to an explanation of how it's going to be done), and sing or at least hum a song a few times through before asking the children to try it.

Like adults, preschool children enjoy singing or hearing "old favorites" again and again; indeed, they have a much higher tolerance for repetition. But if, after a few times of trying a new song, children don't seem interested—drop it; don't try to force their enjoyment.

MATERIALS

	Improvised	Store-bought
Drums	Coffe cans Nail kegs Flower pots, bowls Calfskin, parchment Tacks	Drums—bongo, snare, bass Tom-tom
Sticks	Wooden spoons Tree sticks Cotton, etc. Elastic, string	Drum sticks

Other rhythm
instruments
	Bells, gongs, marimbas
	Horseshoes
	Round tray, lids, etc.
	Tone blocks—blocks of
	  wood
	Sand blocks—sand paper
	  around blocks
	Rattles/shakers—cigar
	  boxes, film containers,
	  canisters, metal boxes
	  filled with nails, pebbles
	Tambourine—paper plate
	  with bells attached
	Barrel hoop with linen and
	  bells
	Cymbals—pie tins, lids
	
	Rhythm sticks—doweling,
	  broom handles
	Triangle—rods of metal
	Thumb piano—hollow
	  sounding board, strips
	  of metal over opening as
	  in guitar
		Gongs, marimbas
		
		Tone blocks
		
		Sand blocks
		
		Rattles
		Jingle clogs
		
		Tambourine
		
		Cymbals (hand and
		  finger)
		Rhythm sticks
		
		Triangle
		Thumb piano

Other accompaniment		Piano Autoharp Recorders Flutes

For suggestions on making your own instruments, read Winn and Porcher, *The Playgroup Book* (1969, pp. 104-107), or an older but equally appropriate book by Mandell and Wood, *Make Your Own Musical Instruments* (1957).

Teachers who lack—or have never developed—musical ability often overemphasize getting children to appreciate "good" music, or they use it to keep children quiet or calm them down. The emphasis ought, instead, to be upon encouraging children to make and move to music. This is the only way they can learn that rhythm (like number) exists everywhere, especially in themselves—that it can take a multitude of forms, and that it is one of man's most powerful means of expression and experience.

ACTIVITIES

The child should "learn" music the way he learns art: by individual, independent exploration. This may go against the grain of many adults, who feel that nothing worthwhile can be done in music without minute attention to detail and much drill, pain, and practice. But with very young children (even older ones, for that matter) the lock-step approach has precisely the same results as the prescriptive, representative approach to art: it turns the child off, out, and away.

Most successful approaches have the following elements in common:

1. *They make a variety of instruments (and records) available to the children to experiment with throughout the day.* It is by handling them and trying them out—much as they handle and try out any other material—that children find out what each instrument can do and how they can use each instrument.

2. *They keep formal large-group activities to a minimum.* While large-group activities are sometimes useful or unavoidable, they are simply not suited to the younger child or to those children of whatever age who find it difficult to be creative or spontaneous in group situations. In music as in other activities, the group situations that work best are those the children set up for themselves.

3. *In general, introduce specific techniques only as a child indicates he needs or wants it.* The point is to make music, not to develop an entire repertoire of individual techniques. Constant interruptions for "demonstrations" by the teacher will kill the children's spontaneous pleasure in music.

4. *Never suggest that there is only one way to play an instrument.* Apart from preventing damage to the instruments, let children experiment at producing new sounds. They might surprise you.

5. *Do not overemphasize records.* An excessive reliance on records inevitably results in canned, impersonal, and passive musical experiences.

Two good discussions of preschool music activities can be found in Chapter 9 of *Understanding Children's Play* (Hartley, Frank & Goldenson, 1952, pp. 298-338) and Elizabeth Jones's National Association for the Education of Young Children booklet entitled *What Is Music for Young Children?* (1969).

RECORDS

Try to listen to any record before you buy it. Your local library is a good place to start. In general, buy those records that you like and that children *can actively respond to* by singing, dancing, and moving. Avoid those that seem too complex or confusing in their mixture of sound, song, and story. American folk songs will probably form the core of your collection. You might also want to include a good sprinkling of Oriental, South American, and African folk songs and instrumental music as well as examples of native American music. Children generally respond well to these, and they suggest musical possibilities that children would not otherwise encounter.

Show the children how to use the phonograph and care for records; as much as possible, give them free access to both during the day.

ACTUAL SOUNDS

Music is a pattern of sound. Hence almost anything that can make a sound can be used as a musical instrument: hands, feet, voices, sticks, or stones. Here are some activities to help children understand that they themselves are musical instruments—and that pianos, guitars, and all other instruments are extensions and elaborations of man's own skills and senses:

1. Trying to make as many different sounds as possible with parts of the body: clapping hands, clapping other parts of the body, stomping feet, clicking heels together.

2. Closing eyes and trying to identify different body sounds.

3. Making body sounds in unison, in rhythm.

The same things can be done with inanimate objects: tapping pencils on the floor, scratching chalk on wood, rubbing sandpaper on wood, or brushing on screen.

RHYTHM ACTIVITIES WITH INSTRUMENTS

Let the children become familiar with the various instruments by using them indoors and out, by themselves or as a part of some activity (dramatic play, for example). Occasionally, when it seems appropriate, suggest different ways of playing an instrument. Take, for example, the following variations with drums:

1. Make different sounds with different drum sticks (soft tipped, hard tipped, no tip).

2. Strike the drum (with different tips) in various places on the skin: the closer to the edge, the tighter the skin and higher the sound.

3. Strike the drum on the edge or the frame.

4. Strike the drum on the skin, then stop the sound with the palm of the hand.

Once the children seem at home with the various instruments, you may want, occasionally, to introduce the following possibilities (preferably to individuals and informal groups):

1. Make alternately loud and soft noises; then, gradual crescendos and decrescendos.

2. Make sounds in various tempos.

3. Make sounds while counting—one-two, one-two, one-two; one-two-three, one-two-three, one-two-three, etc. Later children may want to alternate: one child making a sound at the number one, another child making a sound at number two, and so on. (This introduces the concept of the beat.)

4. Change the accent in a beat (hit one or more sounds hard, the others soft): ONE-two-three, ONE-two-three; ONE-two-THREE-four, ONE-two-THREE-four, etc.

MOVEMENT

Children naturally express themselves by movement. There is always at least one child "dancing" in some way in a preschool. Music and a responsive teacher can encourage more of it and suggest new ideas. Here are some:

1. Introduce songs or recorded music with a strong beat—especially those that they can "act out" or that enable them to imitate animals or trains or the wind, and the like.

2. Include all instruments that need to be shaken and props like scarves, balls, paper streamers that will stimulate movement.

3. Pose questions like, How would you move if you were a wave? or a tree in the wind?

SONGS

Children generally respond to songs with the following characteristics:

1. Simple words and music

2. Repeated phrases and simple rhymes

3. Action: e.g., "She'll Be Coming Round the Mountain" or "Shoo Fly"

4. Silly sounding phrases: "Duck went slishy-sloshy" ("Bought Me a Cat") or "To my wing wong waddle, to my jack straw saddle" ("Swapping Song").

5. Subjects of interest to children: children, animals, transportation, the seasons

6. Relation to immediate activities: trip, rainy day, etc.

Try to introduce songs informally—when an activity suggests a song to you, for example, or sometimes just when everybody seems in the mood for a song. Children pick up songs very quickly—without being drilled.

As with most components of the preschool curriculum, music should be included regularly in the daily program. Children need repetition to build familiarity, to develop confidence in their own ability to experiment and create, and to expand on previous experience.

The teacher should remember, too, that music must not be a purely imitative activity. Just as in art, the teacher should encourage children to project their own feelings through *inventions* rather than *imitation*.

Nature and Science

Wonder, the beginning of knowledge, is also the basis of the young child's approach to the natural world—because it leads him both to explore its variety and to seek to understand its mystery: how things look, sound, change or remain the same, feel, grow. The aim of preschool nature and science activities is primarily to stimulate the child's appreciation of the marvelous variety of his world and his interest in understanding its behavior. More specifically, nature and science activities have the following objectives.

First, they should help children to come to respect the things— especially the living things—of the physical and natural world. They should come to understand that, while plants and trees and animals are there to be used and enjoyed by man, they can be abused.

Second, they should help children understand the *interdependent relationship* between all things in the natural world—especially between man and that world.

Third, they should help children develop a "scientific" approach to the world around them: to observe closely and carefully, to make and test hypotheses, to generalize, and to change their minds on the basis of new evidence.

OUTDOOR ACTIVITIES

Since one aim of the preschool nature and science program is to expose children to as many direct and different experiences of the natural and physical world as possible, they need to take frequent field trips to farms, parks, zoos, and woods—to care

for plants and bushes and animals in the playground and in the classroom.

Field trips can be useless, however, if the teacher does not carefully and deliberately relate them to some objective in the curriculum; field trips are not ends in themselves but opportunities for exposing children to experiences that they cannot encounter within the confines of the classroom or playground. Such excursions do vary the routine and may occasionally be valuable on that account alone; if children are to derive genuine educational benefit from them, however, rather than mere distraction, the teacher must explain their purpose and amplify on the experience before, during, and after the field trip itself.

Suppose, for example, you are taking the children for a walk in the woods and you want to emphasize the varying shapes of leaves, as well as their similarities and their functions. You might, beforehand, let the children look through some simple picture books about leaves, or have them view slides or films, or bring to school leaves they found around their homes. During the walk you will find many occasions to answer their questions about this or that leaf, to ask them questions or suggest possibilities. Give each child a bag on every walk so that he can pick up leaves or anything else that interests him.

After the trip these gatherings can serve as the basis for discussions, for classifying activities, for drawing, and so on. A leaf can be compared with illustrations in a picture book; maybe each child will want to see how many leaves he has that match the illustrations in a book. Perhaps a child may want to "act out" a leaf swaying or tossing in the wind, a leaf opening in the spring or falling in the autumn.

The same kinds of things can be done with stones, birds, animals, with plants in the sun or in the shade (observing and analyzing the different "environments" of sun and shade); the variations depend only on the teacher's ingenuity at using the raw materials of experience and his or her alertness to the signs of interest in the children.

Along with helping a child understand the workings of the natural world, science programs should aim at building the child's respect for the fragileness of life.

Taking care of plants and animals within the school grounds can be a part of the children's regular day-to-day activities. A greenhouse would enable children to work with plants during any season (and understand something of the effect of temperature and sun and moisture as well). Let the children make and tend a garden—preparing the ground, buying (or collecting) seeds, planting them (using labels to mark the spots where different seeds are planted), watering them, and discussing why some have sprouted and some have not, why some have died and some not. A birdhouse, of course, is a natural for a preschool, not only giving the children a sense of pleasurable responsibility for the birds they feed but also opening up possibilities for observations of color, variety, and number: they can count the birds they see; identify them in reference books; draw, paint, and model them; compare their sizes; and discuss why some species appear regularly, while most species never come.

INDOOR ACTIVITIES

Many of the following activities can be conducted outdoors as well as indoors, depending largely on the weather.

AQUARIUM AND TERRARIUM: These can be set up fairly easily; apart from the interest that ''their own'' fish and plants have for children, the tanks serve as miniature models of relatively closed life-support systems, demonstrating the interdependence of animate and inanimate things in a given environment.

ANIMALS: Guinea pigs, hamsters, gerbils, mice, rabbits, birds, toads, and snakes are all suitable preschool pets. Caring for them can build a sense of control and responsibility in children. Chickens are especially stimulating outdoor pets, since they lay eggs which can be eaten or hatched—but they are, unfortunately, too much for most preschools to handle. You might consider hatching a few eggs (obtained from a nearby farm or poultry store) inside the classroom by using an incubator. Work out schedules for care, feeding, carrying out waste, bringing newspapers, cleaning cages, and so on.

PLANTING EXPERIMENTS:

● Plant seeds in a sponge, cotton, paper, a shallow pan with water, or in glass jars filled with water or soil.

• Place a carrot top in a shallow dish with water.

• Plant bulbs in soil in glass jars (keep in a dark room three to five days until roots form, add water, bring into light for blooming).

• Put a sweet potato in a glass jar with water.

• Demonstrate capillary action by putting food dye in a glass of water; add celery, and watch it take on the color of dye.

• Underwater garden: Cover the bottom of a jar with sand; fill with one-half part water, one-half part sodium silicate solution; drop in crystals of ferrous sulphate, zinc sulfide, nickel sulphate, manganese chloride, and cobalt chloride, and watch chemical garden grow.

The bibliography has a number of source materials that the teacher can refer to for other activities.

THE WEATHER

Weather affects children directly, determining what they wear and what they can do, to a much greater extent than it affects adults. It can change swiftly and drastically; consequently, children take weather very personally and will explore it with intense interest. Here are things concerning the weather that children can observe, do, or discuss.

1. *Wind:* The effects it has on other objects—column of smoke, clothes on a line, paper or dust in the street, surface of water, leaves on trees. Its effect on humans: tingling skin, watering eyes, bracing or turning of body or head, running to escape. Experiences with wind: sailing, in a storm, on top of building or mountain. Words about the wind and its effects: what it smells like, sounds like, feels like. Acting out windy scenes. Discussing machines that create wind: fans, hair dryers, even hands.

ACTIVITIES:

• Put a piece of cloth out the window, close the window over one end and observe its reaction to the wind.

• Wash two areas of the chalkboard, fan one with a newspaper and observe difference in drying time.

Top: Science experiments can be long-term projects, but the preschooler will grasp the concepts better if they are broken down into several small but complete units. For instance, the growth of plants from seeds involves a "making planters" stage ... *Opposite page:* a "preparing the planters" stage (which includes gathering the soil and the seeds, and planting the seeds) and ... *Bottom:* a "growing the plants" stage (which includes a daily tending of the crops). Each of these stages can be presented to the child as a separate unit, and then tied together as the whole after the plants have grown—when the child can understand the relationship of each section to the others.

● Make pinwheels and kites and use them in the playground or park.

● Blow toy boats in basin or tub.

2. *Rain:* Effects on objects—changes colors of trees, sidewalks, buildings, collects in puddles in low places, changes dust to mud. Effects on humans—on ordinary clothes and clothes adapted for rain; on people's activities, moods, lives (farmers, construction workers, people going on a picnic); on the natural world. Words for rain and its effects. Where the rain comes from and where it goes (sinks into the earth, evaporates in sun).

3. *Snow:* Similar discussions and investigations can be based on snow. Has anyone lived in a place where there is *no* snow (or where there is snow)? Does that mean they have no Christmas? Are all snowflakes alike? Place on a windowsill a pane of glass or cookie sheet that has been chilled in a freezing compartment and see if the children can note the design of individual flakes before they melt. Use a magnifying glass.

ACTIVITIES:

Assign two children (different ones every evening) to deliver to the class a weather report for the next day—obtained from the newspaper (read to them by parents) or the evening news telecast. Only the essentials, of course: no jargon about "precipitation activity" or "high-pressure zone moving inland." Does the actual weather confirm the forecast? Why would it be important for people to know in advance what the weather will be? Does a change in the weather prevent some people from doing their work? How do changes in the weather affect the clothes that people wear? How does the level of an outside thermometer vary from morning to afternoon? During rain?

SPACE

Study pictures of space and spaceships: make models with cardboard of the sun, moon, earth, and spaceships; draw pictures of these.

ORBITAL GAMES

1. One child stands in the middle of the room holding up a large cardboard model of sun; others move around sun with smaller (to scale) models of stars, earth, moon at varying speeds.

2. Draw the sun on the chalkboard, draw concentric circles around it, and draw various planets and stars on their orbital tracks. Better yet, do this with models on the floor (use blocks or other materials).

PLANETARY MOBILES

1. With fine string, hang various sized cardboard planets painted different colors from single hanger or piece of wire.

2. Attach hangers of various lengths, or pieces of heavy duty wire, to each other at different points. Attach planets to end of each. Watch wind turn each hanger or length of wire around the others.

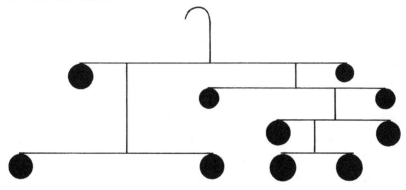

MECHANICAL AND PHYSICAL PRINCIPLES

Make available an array of materials, including the following: flashlight, lock and key, door latch, mechanical tools, magnifying glass, prism, pulleys, scales and weights, suction devices, bell, eggbeater, magnets, mirrors, balloons.

Let children experiment with these materials, offering help as they need it or ask for it.

1. *Magnets (horseshoe, bar):* Set up tray of various objects (wood, metal, plastic). Have the children see which objects the magnet will or will not pick up. Ask them to guess beforehand. After a number of experiments, ask if there is any class of objects the magnet seems to pick up, any class that it does not.

2. *Flashlight:* Compare effect of flashing beam when focused close or far, in light or in dark closet. Place colored paper in front of light; see it make different colors on wall. Try flashing beam through prism and see how direction of the light differs according to point of origin and departure.

3. *Mirrors:* Flash sunlight in different places with a small mirror. Try to trace the beam—is it curved or straight? Stand a pin up in cork, cardboard, or wood; put two small square mirrors on either side of the pin, bend them toward each other, and see the pins multiply. Let children experiment with both curved and flat mirrors. Let them look at their reflections on both sides of a large, clear silver spoon.

4. *Magnifying (light refraction):* Partially fill glasses and bowls with water; let children put fingers, pencils, straws inside and view from the outside—submerged part will look larger and object will look broken. Let children experiment and see how different things look through curved and flat transparent glass, through glass and water, and through glass alone.

5. *Shadows:* Let children throw shadows on wall from light of lamp using objects held up to light, finger shapes, and head. Let the children trace shapes on paper. As objects move toward or away from light, do the shadows get smaller or bigger? What does this say about light? (That it travels in a straight line.) Experiment with objects of varying degrees of opaqueness or transparency (demonstrates that shadows are made when an object blocks out light).

Let children measure their shadows outside at different times of the day to see when shadows are longest and shortest, and how they change directions. With a flashlight, they can experiment with changing the length and direction of shadows of various objects. Make a crude sundial: stand a pencil in a small box filled with clay. Put the box in a window, where it will receive sunlight. Notice how the shadow moves during the day.

6. *Pulleys:* Get single and double pulleys and lengths of clothesline. Arrange different pulley systems. Knot free end of line so it won't slip; use paper clips as hooks. Let children lift objects of different weights with different pulley systems and discover that the same object seems lighter with one pulley system than with another.

7. *Balloons:* Let children (on cold, clear day) rub blown-up balloons on clothes and place them against a wall to see if they will stay. Or let them rub balloons in their hair and see if they will stay on their arm. By blowing up balloons and then letting them go, children can discover the principle of jet propulsion.

Many "science" experiences occur during the course of other activities—water play, for example, and cooking. By asking the right questions at the right time, the teacher can encourage scientific curiosity.

Conclusion

This book has attempted to stress the importance of appropriate preschooling. Nursery schools, day-care centers, and other similar institutions may offer parents and society ancillary values by providing supervision for young children who would otherwise lack it, or by injecting some element of play and pleasure into otherwise chaotic or grim young lives.

Desirable as these other values are, and socially imperative as they may be in some cases, the practitioner should not allow them to obscure the core idea that the preschool years are those in which the human mind develops most rapidly and learns with the greatest pleasure and the least effort. This fact—and it is sufficiently backed by enough research to call it a fact rather than an hypothesis—holds out two great possibilities to us: first, that the wise use of the preschool years can help us provide a rich, stimulating environment that could greatly enhance the positive maturation of future generations; second, that effective preschooling can raise the intellectual functioning of those children whom we term *disadvantaged*.

At present, however, there is a great and often frustrating disparity between possibility and reality. Unanimous as the research findings are on the importance of the early, preschool years to human development, the findings on the specific preschool programs are scattered, inconclusive, and even contradictory. A well-publicized study of Head Start, for example, indicated that

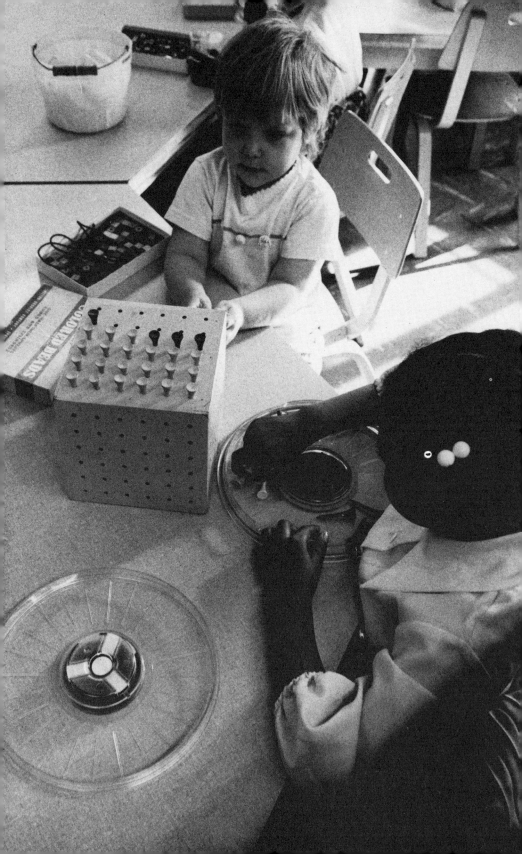

while children in the program registered some initial gains over control-group children outside the program, those gains disappeared soon after both groups entered regular school.

A great part of the difficulty, I suspect, lies in the fact that most elementary schools are not organized or equipped to individualize the instructional program and take advantage of these early year experiences. Neither has appropriate recognition been given to the influence of the home environment on young children nor have programs been organized to include involved activities for the home.

Statements in the above paragraph are guesses, offered without benefit of adequate research. Many other hypotheses have been offered to explain the failure of preschool programs to live up to the expectations of their adult sponsors. Some of them, it seems to me, are rather desperate attempts to find *some* value in a program regardless of unfavorable evaluation results—the educational equivalent of changing the scoring rules of a game after it's been played to make sure that your team wins. But others are plausible, part of the inevitable trial-error process by which we design a program according to the best information available, test it, and begin revising it to maximize the gains and minimize the losses.

The most reliable conclusion to be drawn from our experiments with early childhood education is that we do not know nearly enough about human growth and development during these early years. In addition, as many childhood experts point out, we may have to rethink our stated objectives. Is academic success as we measure it during the years of formal education the most important objective to shoot for in the preschool years? Or, are other outcomes that we do not evaluate equally desirable—for example, a growing sense of confidence in one's ability, a pure sense of pleasure in discovering the wonderful variety of the world, a chance to explore one's personal interests before the

In the preschool years, children are most likely to learn with the least effort and the most pleasure.

Following pages: **Learning is the business of the young, and it is our business to provide places and times where and when learning can best take place.**

academic curriculum imposes society's interests on the child. At present, many if not most preschool programs are operated in virtual isolation from the public and private schools that will continue the child's education in later years; if the effectiveness of preschooling is to be measured by the child's record in these other, unconnected institutions, it may be necessary to develop new patterns of cooperation between the personnel of both to improve the compatibility of their respective efforts—that is, to make sure that preschool programs lead logically into school programs and that children are placed at their appropriate ability levels regardless of age. If we do that, however, if we say that preschooling is not successful unless it clearly helps the child succeed in school, we may appropriately ask how effective school programs are in achieving what *they* presume to do. There is very little correlation between school grades and success in life, whether "success in life" be equated with earning a large income, achieving fame, finding fulfillment in an occupation, or making a happy marriage. And if the schools fail to achieve success in *their* stated goals with any regularity, how important is it that the preschool tailor its goals to increase the likelihood of high grades?

At this point, the reader may wonder whether, with all these questions, there is anything we *do* know about early childhood.

Yes. It would appear that the years from birth to five and the activities (or lack of) the youngster is exposed to and participates in during these years are extremely important to the maturation of the human mind. Interesting and stimulating early childhood experiences do make a difference.

It would appear that children placed under stress to achieve certain educative goals, and for which these children have not as yet reached a point of proper physical and mental maturation (the problem of the match), can be damaged emotionally and physically. It would also appear that early involvement with the home environment of a youngster and the continuing association with the home has a very positive impact on both the home and the ECE program for a young child.

We know enough, in short, to justify a major investment of

further research in this field, and of carefully evaluated development efforts to narrow the continuing gap between intention and
result in preschool programs. Yet we cannot wait until all our
questions are answered before acting on the best blend of knowledge, experience, and experiment that we can fashion now. We
cannot defer all action until our information is perfect; indeed,
it is important to remember that, in education as well as in
virtually every other sphere of life, we often learn *in the process*
of acting.

The learning-through-discovery perspective discussed in this
book offers to teachers a highly flexible, child-centered preschool
program that allows children to pursue their own interests. It
is rooted in the conviction that the spontaneous, unforced interests
of children naturally lead them up paths of intellectual growth
and that their progress up those paths can be accelerated by
intelligent, perceptive, interested adults.

BIBLIOGRAPHY

Aaron, David, and Bonnie P. Winawer. *Child's Play: A Creative Approach to Playspaces for Today's Children*. New York: Harper & Row, 1965.

Abeson, Marion. *Playtime with Music*. New York: Liveright, 1967.

Abramson, Paul. *Schools for Early Childhood*. New York: Educational Facilities Laboratories, 1970.

Agee, Kate K. "Monoprinting." *Grade Teacher,* vol. 87, p. 52, 1969.

Allstrom, Elizabeth. *You Can Teach Creatively*. Nashville, Tenn.: Abingdon, 1970.

Almy, Millie. "What Can Children Learn in Nursery School?" *Journal of Nursery Education,* vol. 17, no. 3, pp. 137-140, 1962.

——. *Young Children Thinking*. New York: Teachers College, 1966.

Alton, W. G. *Woodwork Projects*. New York: Taplinger, 1967.

——. *More Woodwork Projects*. New York: Taplinger, 1969.

American Association for Health, Physical Education and Recreation. *Promising Practices in Elementary School Physical Education*. Washington, D.C., 1969.

Anderson, Robert H., and Harold G. Shane, eds. *As the Twig Is Bent: Readings in Early Childhood Education*. Boston: Houghton Mifflin, 1971.

Andrews, F. Emerson. *Numbers Please*. Boston: Little, Brown, 1961.

Andrews, Gladys. *Creative Rhythmic Movement for Children*. Englewood Cliffs, N.J.: Prentice-Hall, 1954.

Antin, Clara. *Blocks in the Curriculum*. New York: Early Childhood Education Council. n.d.

Ashton-Warner, Sylvia. *Teacher*. New York: Simon & Schuster, 1963.

Association for Childhood Education International. *Art for Children's Growing*. Washington, D.C., n.d.

——. *Equipment & Supplies*. Washington, D.C., 1965.

——. *Housing for Early Childhood Education*. Washington, D.C., 1968.

——. "Learning from Parents." *Childhood Education,* March 1971, pp. 135-137.

——. *Music for Children's Living*. Washington, D.C., 1955.

——. *Nursery School Portfolio*. Washington, D.C., 1951.

——. *Play–Children's Business: Guide to Selection of Toys and Games,*

Infants to Twelve Years Old. Washington, D.C., 1963.

————. *Young Children and Science.* Washington, D.C., 1964.

Association for Supervision and Curriculum Development, National Education Association. "Early Childhood Education: A Perspective." *Educational Leadership,* May 1971, pp. 788-831.

Bailey, Charity. "Music and the Beginning School Child." *Young Children,* vol. 21, no. 4, pp. 200-204.

Baker, Katherine Read, and Xenia F. Fane. *Understanding and Guiding Young Children.* Englewood Cliffs, N. J.: Prentice-Hall, 1970.

Baker, Katherine Read, ed. *Ideas that Work with Young Children.* Washington, D.C.: National Association for the Education of Young Children, 1972.

Bannon, Laura. *Mind Your Child's Art.* New York: Pellegrini & Cudahy, 1952.

Barker, Will. *Freshwater Friends and Foes.* Washington, D.C.: Acropolis, 1966.

Barnouw, Elsa, and Arthur Swan. *Air, Wind and Weather.* New York: Holt, 1958 .

————. *Adventures with Children in Nursery School and Kindergarten.* New York: Agathon Press, 1970.

Barlett, M.G. "Water, Water." *Grade Teacher,* vol. 81, no. 1, p. 18, 1963.

————. "Light and Shadow." *Grade Teacher,* vol. 81, no. 2, p. 20, 1963.

————. "Weather and Kindergartens." *Grade Teacher,* vol. 81, no. 7, p. 16, 1964.

Bateman, Barbara. *The Essentials of Teaching and Temporal Learning.* Dimensions in Early Learning Series. San Rafael, Calif.: Dimensions Publishing Co., 1966.

————. *Temporal Learning.* Dimensions in Early Learning Series. San Rafael, Calif.: Dimensions Publishing Co., 1966.

Beard, Ruth M. *An Outline of Piaget's Developmental Psychology for Students and Teachers.* New York: Basic Books, 1969.

Bereiter, Carl. *Arithmetic and Mathematics.* Dimensions in Early Learning Series. San Rafael, Calif.: Dimensions Publishing Co., 1968.

————, and Siegried Engelmann. *Teaching Disadvantaged Children in the Preschool.* Englewood Cliffs, N.J.: Prentice-Hall, 1966.

Bernstein, Basil. "Language and Social Class." *British Journal of Sociology,* vol. 11, pp. 271-276, 1960.

Berson, Minnie P. *Individualizing Instruction.* Chicago: The University of Chicago Press, 1962.

Beyer, Evelyn. *Teaching Young Children.* New York: Pegasus, 1968.

Biber, Barbara. *Challenges Ahead for Early Childhood Education.* Washington, D.C.: National Association for the Education of Young Children, 1969.

————. *Children's Drawings.* New York: Bank Street Publications, 1963.

————. Edna Shapiro, and David Wickens. *Promoting Cognitive Growth.* Washington, D.C.: National Association for the Education of Young Children, 1971.

Biemiller, Andrew J., ed. *Problems in the Teaching of Young Children.* Monograph series no. 9. Toronto: The Ontario Institute for Studies in Education, 1970.

Bloom, Benjamin. *Stability and Change in Human Characteristics.* New York: Wiley, 1964.

Blough, Glenn O., Julius Schwartz, and Albert J. Huggett. *Elementary School Science and How to Teach It.* New York: Holt, 1958.

Blum, Licille H., and Anna Dragositz. "Finger-Painting: Developmental Aspects." *Child Development,* vol. 18, no. 3, pp. 88-105, 1947.

Bogtrykkeri, Nordlundes. *Space for Play.* World Organization for Early Childhood Education, 1964.

Bosse, Murella. "They Grow with Music." *Instructor,* vol. 78, p. 40, 1969.

Boy Scouts of America. *Woodwork.* New Brunswick, N.J., 1952.

Braley, William T., Geraldine Konicki, and Catherine Leedy. *Daily Sensorimotor Training Activities—A Handbook for Teachers and Parents of Pre-school Children.* Freeport, N.Y.: Educational Activities, Inc., 1968.

Brearley, Molly, et al. *The Teaching of Young Children: Some Applications of Piaget's Learning Theory.* New York: Schocken Books, 1970.

Brittain, W. L. "Some Exploratory Studies of the Art of Pre-school Children." *Studies in Art Education,* vol. 10, pp. 14-24. 1969.

Bronfenbrenner, Urie. *Two Worlds of Childhood: U.S. and U.S.S.R.* New York: Basic Books, 1970.

————, et al. *Two Worlds of Childhood: U.S. and U.S.S.R.* New York: Russell Sage Foundation, 1970.

Brown, Bob. *Science Treasures: Let's Repeat the Great Experiments.* New York: Fleet Press, 1968.

Brown, Doris V., and Pauline McDonald. *Creative Art Activities for Home and School.* Los Angeles: Lawrence Publishing Co., 1966.

Brown, Roger. *Words and Things*. Glencoe, Ill.: Free Press, 1958.

Bruce, D. J. "Analysis of Word Sounds by Young Children." *British Journal of Educational Psychology,* vol. 34, pp. 158-170, 1964.

Bruner, Jerome. *The Process of Education*. Cambridge, Mass.: Harvard University Press, 1960.

———. *Toward a Theory of Instruction*. Cambridge, Mass.: Harvard, 1966.

Buck, Margaret Waring. *Along the Seashore*. Nashville, Tenn.: Abingdon, 1964.

———. *In Ponds and Streams*. Nashville, Tenn.: Abingdon, 1955.

———. *In Yards and Gardens*. Nashville, Tenn.: Abingdon, 1952.

———. *Small Pets from Fields and Streams*. Nashville, Tenn.: Abingdon, 1960.

Buktenica, Norman. *Visual Learning*. Dimensions in Early Learning Series. San Rafael, Calif.: Dimensions Publishing Co., 1966.

Burns, Sylvia E. "Children Respond to Improvised Equipment." *Young Children,* vol. 20, no. 1, pp. 28-38, 1964.

Buttolph, Edna. *Music for the Classroom Teacher*. New York: Bank Street College, 1958.

———. *Music with Young Children*. New York: Bank Street College, n.d.

Caldwell, Bettye. "What Is the Optimal Learning Environment for the Young Child?" *American Journal of Orthopsychiatry,* January 1967, pp. 8-21.

California State Department of Education. *Implementing Mathematics Programs in California: A Guide: K-8*. Menlo Park, Calif.: State Department of Education, 1965.

Cannon, Gwendolyn McConkie. "Kindergarten Class Size—A Study." *Childhood Education,* vol. 43, no. 1, pp. 9-13, 1966.

Caplan, Frank, and Theresa Caplan. *The Power of Play*. Garden City, N.J.: Anchor Books, Doubleday & Company, Inc., 1973.

Carona, Philip B. *Water*. Chicago: Follett, 1966.

Chall, Jeanne S. *Learning to Read: The Great Debate*. New York: McGraw-Hill, 1967.

Chandler, M. H. *Science and the World around Us*. Chicago: Rand McNally, 1968.

Chauncey, Henry, and Educational Testing Service, eds. *Soviet Preschool Education*. Vol. I. Program of Instruction. New York: Holt, 1969.

Cherry, Clare. *Creative Movement for the Developing Child: A Nursery School Handbook for Non-musicians.* Palo Alto, Calif.: Fearon, 1968.

Children's Museum. *Water Play: Materials and Activities for Teachers and Children. Match Box Project.* Boston: The Children's Museum, 1967.

Chomsky, Carol. *The Acquisition of Syntax in Children Five to Ten.* Cambridge, Mass.: M.I.T., 1970.

Christianson, Helen, Mary M. Rogers, and Blanche A. Ludium. *The Nursery School, Adventures in Living and Learning.* Boston: Houghton Mifflin, 1961.

Chukovsky, Kornei. *From Two to Five.* Berkeley: University of California Press, 1968.

Church, Joseph. *Language and the Discovery of Reality.* New York: Random House, 1961.

Cieslinski, Anita. *Preschool Math.* Columbus, Ohio: Merrill, 1967.

Clarke, Arthur C. *Man and Space.* New York: Time-Life, 1968.

Cohen, D. H. "Language and Experience: The Setting." *Childhood Education,* vol. 42, no. 3, pp. 139-142, 1965.

Cohen, Monroe D., ed. *A Lap to Sit On . . .and Much More.* Washington, D.C.: Association for Childhood Education International, 1971.

Colton, E. V. "Art as a Language." *School Arts,* vol. 69, pp. 14-15, 1969.

Contemporary Education. "New Concepts for Sand and Water Play Introduced for Young Children: Martian Canals." *Contemporary Education,* vol. 40, p. 182, 1969.

Cooper, Elizabeth. *Science in Your Own Backyard.* New York: Harcourt, Brace, 1958.

Corcoran, A. L. "Color Usage in Nursery School Painting." *Child Development,* vol. 25, no. 2, pp. 107-113, 1954.

Cornelius, Ruth. "Art—A Way of Life." *Childhood Education,* vol. 40, no. 6, pp. 283-285, 1964.

Cottle, Thomas J. *Black Children, White Dreams.* Boston: Houghton Mifflin, 1974.

Cypreansen, Lucile. "Listening as a Skill." *Childhood Education,* vol. 37, no. 6, pp. 268-270, 1961.

Davis, D. C. "Play: A State of Childhood." *Childhood Education,* vol. 42, no. 4, pp. 242-244, 1965.

Davis, R. B. *The Changing Curriculum: Mathematics.* Washington, D.C.: Association for Supervision and Curriculum Development, 1967.

Dawson, M. A., and G. C. Newman. *Learning Teaching in Kindergarten and The Early Primary Grades.* New York: Harcourt, Brace & World, 1966.

Day, M. M. "Very Young in Art." *School Arts,* vol. 69, pp. 30-31, 1969.

Deal, T. N., and J. P. Maness. "New Horizons in Kindermath." *Young Children,* vol. 23, pp. 354-357, 1968.

DeHirsch, Katrinia. "Preschool Intervention." *Reading Forum,* National Institute of Neurological Diseases and Stroke. Monograph 11. Washington, D.C.: U.S. Government Printing Office, 1971.

Denner, Patricia. *Language through Play.* New York: Arno, New York Times, 1969.

Durkin, Dolores, *Children Who Read Early.* New York: Teachers College, Columbia University, 1966.

―――. "Should the Very Young Be Taught to Read?" *NEA Journal,* vol. 52, no. 3, pp. 20-23, 1963.

Education Commission of the States, Task Force on Early Childhood Education. *Early Childhood Development: Alternatives for Program Implementation in the States.* Denver, 1971.

Educational Facilities Laboratory. *Schools without Walls.* New York, 1965.

Elkind, David. "Children's Discovery of the Conservation of Mass, Weight and Volume: Piaget Replication Study II." *Journal of Genetic Psychology,* vol. 98, pp. 219-227, 1961.

―――. "The Development of the Additive Composition of Classes in the Child: Piaget Replication Study III." *Journal of Genetic Psychology,* vol. 99, pp. 51-57, 1961.

―――. "The Development of Quantitative Thinking: A Systematic Replication of Piaget's Studies." *Journal of Genetic Psychology,* vol. 98, pp. 37-46, 1961.

―――. "Discrimination, Seriation, and Numeration of Size & Dimensional Difference in Young Children: Piaget Replication Study VI." *Journal of Genetic Psychology,* vol. 104, pp. 275-296, 1964.

Ellis, Mary J., and Frances Lyons. *Finger Playtime.* Minneapolis: T. S. Denison, 1960.

Endicott, Robert F. *Scrap Wood Fun for Kids.* New York: Association Press, 1961.

Engelmann, Siegfried. *Conceptual Learning.* Dimensions in Early Learning Series. San Rafael, Calif.: Dimensions Publishing Co., 1966.

―――, and Therese Englemann. *Give Your Child a Superior Mind.* New York: Simon and Schuster, 1966.

————, and Therese Englemann. *Preventing Failure in the Primary Grades.* Chicago: Science Research Associates, 1969.

————, et al. *Learning Language.* Vols. 1–3. Urbana: University of Illinois Press, 1968.

Enthoven, Jacqueline. *Stitchery for Children: A Manual for Teachers.* New York: Van Nostrand Reinhold, 1968.

Erikson, Erik. *Childhood and Society.* New York: Norton, 1951.

Erwin, Gerald W. *Music for Everyone.* State of Hawaii: Department of Public Instruction, 1959.

Feshbach, Norma C., John I. Goodlad, and Avima Lombard. *Early Schooling in England and Israel.* |I|D|E|A| Reports on Schooling (Early Schooling Series). New York: McGraw-Hill, 1973.

Fletcher, Helen Jill. *Children's Dances Around the World.* Darien, Conn.: Educational Publishing Co., 1961.

Forbes, Jack E. *Mathematical Skills: Developmental Program.* Chicago: Systems for Education, Inc., 1965.

Fowler, William. *Infant Stimulation and the Etiology of Cognitive Processes.* Toronto: Ontario Institute for Studies in Education, 1971.

Frank, L. K. "The Role of Play in Child Development." *Childhood Education,* vol. 41, no. 2, pp. 70-73, 1964.

Franklin, Adele. *Blocks—A Tool of Learning.* New York: Bank Street College, n.d.

Freidus, Elizabeth. *Writing.* Dimensions in Early Learning Series. San Rafael, Calif.: Dimensions Publishing Co., 1966.

Frisch, Rose E. *Plants that Feed the World.* New York: Van Nostrand Reinhold, 1966.

Frost, J. L. *Issues and Innovations in the Teaching of Reading.* Glenview, Ill.: Scott, Foresman, 1967.

Frostig, Marianne. *Frostig Program for Development of Vision Perception.* Chicago: Follett, 1964.

Furth, Hans C. *Piaget for Teachers.* Englewood Cliffs, N.J.: Prentice-Hall, 1969.

Gagne, Robert M. *The Conditions of Learning.* New York: Holt, 1965.

Gaitskell, Charles D. *Children and Their Art.* New York: Harcourt, Brace, 1958.

Gesell, Arnold. *The Mental Growth of the Preschool Child.* St. Clare Shores, Mich.: Scholarly Press, 1925.

Giambarba, Paul. *What Is It? At the Beach.* Barre, Mass.: Scrimshaw Press, 1969.

Gibson, John. *Citizenship.* Dimensions in Early Learning Series. San Rafael, Calif.: Dimensions Publishing Co., 1966.

Goodlad, John I., M. Frances Klein, Jerrold M. Novotney, and associates. *Early Schooling in the United States.* |I|D|E|A| Reports on Schooling (Early Schooling Series). New York: McGraw-Hill, 1973.

Gordon, Ira J. *Human Development: From Birth through Adolescence.* New York: Harper & Row, 1969.

––––––. *On Early Learning: The Modifiability of Human Potential.* Washington, D.C.: Association for Supervision and Curriculum Development, 1971.

––––––. *Studying the Child in the School.* New York: Wiley, 1966.

Green, Marjorie, and Elizabeth Woods. *A Nursery School Handbook.* Sierra Madre, Calif.: Sierra Madre Community Nursery School Association, 1963.

––––––. *A Nursery School Handbook for Teachers and Parents.* Sierra Madre, Calif.: Sierra Madre Community Nursery School Association, 1961.

Greenlee, Julian. *Teaching Science to Children.* Dubuque, Iowa: Wm. C. Brown, 1957.

Griffin-King, June. *Making and Creating with Everyday Materials.* Newton Centre, Mass.: Branford, 1969.

Gross, Ronald, and Judith Murphy. *Educational Change & Architectural Consequences.* New York: Educational Facilities Laboratories, 1968.

Guillaume, Jeanette. "Water, Water Everywhere." *Parents Magazine,* August 1959, p. 50.

Haase, Ronald W. *Designing the Child Development Center.* Washington, D.C.: Project Head Start. United States Office of Economic Opportunity, 1969.

Hackett, Layne C., and Robert G. Jenson. *A Guide to Movement Exploration.* Palo Alto, Calif.: Peck Publications, 1966.

Hamlin and Guessoford. *Singing Games for Children.* Cincinnati, Ohio: The Willis Music Co., n.d.

Haring, Norris. *Attending and Responding.* Dimensions in Early Learning Series. San Rafael, Calif.: Dimensions Publishing Co., 1966.

Hartley, Ruth. *Complete Book of Children's Play.* New York: Thomas Y. Crowell, 1963.

Hartley, Ruth, L. K. Frank, and R. M. Goldenson. *Understanding Children's Play.* New York: Columbia University Press, 1952.

Hartup, Willard, and Nancy Smothergill, eds. *The Young Child: Reviews of Research.* Washington, D.C.: National Association for the Education of Young Children, 1967.

Harvey, Mary Martha Woodward. "Glue-Stick-Balance-Dry: Toothpick Sculpture." *Arts and Activities,* vol. 66, p. 26, 1969.

Harvey, Sister Ann. *Rhythm and Dances for Preschool and Kindergarten.* New York: Schirmer, n.d.

Hasterok, Gerald. *Memory.* Dimensions in Early Learning Series. San Rafael, Calif.: Dimensions Publishing Co., 1966.

Hatcher, Caro C., and Hilda Mullin. *More Than Words: Movement Activities for Children.* Pasadena, Calif.: Parents-for-Movement Publication, 1967.

Haupt, Dorothy, and D. Keith Osborn. *Creative Activities for Young Children.* Detroit: Merrill-Palmer Institute of Human Development and Family Life, 1964.

Hayward, Charles H. *Junior Woodworker.* Mystic, Conn.: Verry, Lawrence, Inc., 1973.

Heard, I. M. "Making and Using Graphs in the Kindergarten Mathematics Program." *Arithmetic Teacher,* vol. 15, pp. 504-506, 1968.

———. "Number Games with Young Children." *Young Children,* vol. 24, pp. 146-150, 1969.

Heidt, A. H. "Crayon Cover-Up." *Arts and Activities,* May 1969, pp. 24-26.

Hess, Robert D., and Anita Meyer Bear, eds. *Early Education: Current Theory, Research and Action.* Chicago: Aldine, 1968.

Hess, Robert D., and Doreen J. Croft. *Teachers of Young Children.* Boston: Houghton Mifflin, 1972.

Hewes, Jeremy Joan. *Build Your Own Playground!* Boston: San Francisco Book Company/Houghton Mifflin, 1974.

Highlights Editors. *Creative Craft Activities.* Jumbo Handbook Series. New York, 1967.

Hill, Katherine E. "Science for Children—Why?" *Science and Children,* vol. 3, no. 8, pp. 11-12, 1966.

Hoagey, C. Y. "Birds in Spring." *Instructor,* vol. 77, p. 33, 1968.

———. "Finger Fun." *Instructor,* vol. 77, p. 39, 1968.

Hochman, Vivienne, and Mildred Greenwald. *Science Experiences in Early Childhood Education.* New York: Bank Street College, 1969.

Hoffman, David B., et al. *Parent Participation in Preschool Day Care.* Atlanta, Ga.: Southwest Educational Development Laboratory, 1971.

Holmes, Emma E. *Mathematics Instruction for Children.* Belmont, Calif.: Wadsworth, 1968.

Holt, John. *How Children Fail.* New York: Pitman, 1967.

———. *How Children Learn.* New York: Pitman, 1969.

Hoover, F. Louis. *Art Activities for the Very Young.* Worcester, Mass.: Davis Publications, Inc., 1969.

Howard, Norma K., comp. *Day Care: An Annotated Bibliography.* Urbana, Ill.: ERIC, Clearinghouse on Early Childhood Education, 1971.

Hromadka, Van G. *Child Development Guides for Teachers of Three-, Four-, and Five-Year Old Children.* Albany, N.Y.: State Education Department, 1957.

Hunt, J. Mc Vicker. *The Challenges of Incompetence and Poverty.* Urbana: The University of Illinois Press, 1969.

————. *Intelligence and Experiences.* New York: Ronald, 1961.

————. "Parent and Child Centers: Their Basis in the Behavioral and Educational Sciences." *American Journal of Orthopsychiatry,* vol. 41, pp. 13-38, 1971.

Hymes, James L., Jr. *Before the Child Reads.* White Plains, N.Y.: Row, Peterson, 1958.

————. *Teaching the Child Under Six.* Columbus, Ohio: Merrill, 1974.

Ilg, F. L., and L. B. Ames. *School Readiness.* New York: Harper & Row, 1964.

Inbody, Donald. "Children's Understanding of Natural Phenomenon." *Science Education,* vol. 47, no. 3, pp. 270-278, 1963.

————. "Kindergarten and First Grade Science." *Science and Children,* vol. 1, no. 4, pp. 26–28, 1963.

Institute for Development of Educational Activities, Inc. *The British Infant School.* Vol. I. Early Childhood Series. Melbourne, Fla.: 1969.

————. *Influence of Home Environment on the Success of First Graders as Viewed by Mothers of First Grade Students.* Dayton, Ohio, 1969.

————. *Influence of Home Environment on the Success of First Graders as Viewed by Teachers of First Grade.* Dayton, Ohio, 1969.

International Council for Health, Physical Education and Recreation. *Book of Worldwide Games and Dances.* Washington, D.C.: American Association for Health, Physical Education and Recreation, National Education Association, n.d.

Irwin, O. C. "Acceleration of Infant Speech by Story-Reading." *Behavior in Infancy and Early Childhood.* Edited by Brackbill and Thompson. New York: Free Press, 1967.

Isaacs, Nathan. *(Studies of Piaget) New Light on Ideas of Numbers.* London: Ward Locke Educational Supply Association, 1964.

Isaacs, Susan. *The Nursery Years.* New York: Schocken Books, 1968.

Ivancevich, Judy. "Art Is Individual." *Instructor,* vol. 79, pp. 145-146, 1969.

Jacobs, Frances E. *Finger Plays and Action Rhymes.* New York: Lothrop, Lee & Shepart Co., 1941.

Jameson, Kenneth. *Art and the Young Child.* New York: Viking, 1969.

Jenkins, Ella. *The Ella Jenkins Song Book for Children.* New York: Oak Publications, Inc., 1966.

————. *This Is Rhythm.* New York: Oak Publications, Inc. 1962.

Jensen, Arthur R. *Understanding Readiness: An Occasional Paper.* Urbana, Ill.: ERIC Clearinghouse on Early Childhood Education, 1969.

John, Vera P., and Vivian M. Horner. *Early Childhood Bilingual Education.* New York: Modern Language Association, 1971.

Jones, Elizabeth. *What Is Music for Young Children?* Washington, D.C.: National Association for the Education of Young Children, 1969.

Jones, Richard E. *Contemporary Educational Psychology.* New York: Harper & Row, 1967.

Kagan, Jerome. "Cross-Cultural Perspectives on Early Development." Address to American Association for the Advancement of Science, December 26, 1972.

Kames, Merle. *Helping Young Children Develop Language Skills.* Washington, D.C.: Council for Exceptional Children, 1968.

Kellogg, Rhoda, with Scott O'Dell. *The Psychology of Children's Art.* Del Mar, Calif.: Communications Research Machines, Inc., Random House, 1967.

Kepler, Hazel. *The Child and His Play.* New York: Funk & Wagnalls, 1952.

Kirchner, Glenn, Jean Cunningham, and Eileen Warrell. *Introduction to Movement Education: An Individualized Approach to Teaching.* Dubuque, Iowa: W. C. Brown, 1970.

Kohn, Sherwood. *The Early Learning Center.* New York: Educational Facilities Laboratories, 1970.

Kraus, Philip E. *Yesterday's Children.* New York: Wiley-Interscience, 1973.

Krauzer, Herman C. *Nature and Science Activities for Young Children.* Jenkintown, Pa.: Baker Publishing Co., 1969.

Krevitsky, Nik. *Stitchery.* New York: Reinhold, 1966.

Krone, Beatrice, and Kurt R. Miller. *Help Yourselves to Music.* San Francisco: H. Chandler, 1959.

Kutchevsky, Sybil, and Elizabeth Prescott. *Planning Environments for Young Children.* Washington, D.C.: National Association for the Education of Young Children, 1969.

Landeck, Beatrice. *Children and Music: An Informal Guide for Parents and Teachers*. New York: E. B. Marks Music Corp., 1952

————, ed. *More Songs to Grow On*. New York: E. B. Marks Music Corp., 1954.

————, ed. *Songs to Grow On*. New York: Sloane, 1950.

Larrick, Nancy. *A Parent's Guide to Children's Reading*. New York: Pocket Books, 1969.

Lavatelli, Celia S. *Piaget's Theory and Early Childhood Curriculum*. Boston: American Science & Engineering, 1970.

Law, Norma R. *Outdoor Play for Young Children*. Washington, D.C.: Association for Childhood Education International, 1965.

————, and Hui C. Wu. "Equipment: Challenge or Sterotype?" *Young Children,* vol. 20, no. 1, pp. 18-24, 1964.

Leacock, Eleanor Burke. *Teaching and Learning in City Schools: A Comparative Study*. New York: Basic Books, 1969.

Leavitt, Jerome E. *Carpentry for Children*. New York: Sterling, 1959.

Leeming, Joseph. *Fun with Wood*. Philadelphia: Lippincott, 1942.

Leeper, Sarah Hammond, et al. *Good Schools for Young Children*. New York: Macmillan, 1968.

Lewis, Claudia. *Language as an Art*. New York: Bank Street College, n.d.

Lincoln, Martha, and Katharine Torrey. *The Workshop Book for Parents and Children*. Boston: Houghton Mifflin, 1955.

Lindeman, Earl W., and Donald W. Herberholz. *Developing Artistic and Perceptual Awareness*. Dubuque, Iowa: Wm. C. Brown, 1964.

Lindstrom, Miriam. *Children's Art*. Berkeley, Calif.: University of California Press, 1957.

Locke, O. C. "Do Children Need to Draw?" *School Arts,* vol. 68, pp. 6-7, 1969.

Loeffler, Margaret Howard. *The Prepared Environment*. Oklahoma City: Casady School, 1968.

Logan, Lillian. *Teaching the Young Child Methods of Preschool and Primary Education*. Boston: Houghton Mifflin, 1960.

Los Angeles City Schools. *Learning to Move—Moving to Learn: Movement Exploration and Discovery*. Publication No. EC-260. Los Angeles: Division of Instructional Planning and Services, 1968.

Lovell, Kenneth. *The Growth of Basic Mathematical and Scientific Concepts in Children*. London: University of London Press, Ltd., 1962.

McCall, Adeline. *This Is Music for Kindergarten and Nursery School.* Boston: Allyn and Bacon, 1965.

McCarthy, Dorothea. "Language Development in Children." *Manual of Child Psychology.* Edited by Leonard Carmichael. New York: Wiley, 1954.

McCarthy, Jan, and Charles R. May, eds. *Providing the Best for Young Children.* Washington, D.C.: National Association for the Education of Young Children, 1974.

McFee, June F. *Preparation for Art.* San Francisco, Calif.: Wadsworth, 1961.

Mandell, Muriel, and Robert E. Wood. *Make Your Own Musical Instruments.* New York: Sterling, 1957.

Mankin, Linda. "Are We Starting Too Late? Preschool Music Education." *Music Educators Journal,* vol. 55, pp. 36-40, 1969.

Marks, J. L., C. R. Purdy, and L. B. Kinney. *Teaching Elementary School Mathematics for Understanding.* New York: McGraw-Hill, 1970.

Matterson, E. M. *Play and Playthings for the Preschool Child.* Baltimore: Penguin, 1968.

May, Lola. *Modern Math, Grade by Grade (K).* Darien, Conn.: Teachers Publishing Corp., n.d.

Mead, Margaret. *A Creative Life for Your Children.* Washington, D.C.: U.S. Government Printing Office, 1966.

Meilach, Dona Z. *Creating Art from Anything: Ideas, Materials and Techniques.* Chicago: Reilly & Lee, 1968.

Meindl, M. G. "Rainpaint." *Arts and Activities,* vol. 66, p. 40, 1969.

Mendelowitz, Daniel M. *Children Are Artists.* Stanford, Calif.: Stanford, 1953.

Merrill, Lindsey, "Where Do Our Children Lose Their Ears?" *Music Journal,* vol. 24, no. 3, pp. 57, 116-117, 1966.

Michael, William B. *Teaching for Creative Endeavor: Bold New Venture.* Bloomington: Indiana University Press, 1968.

Millan, Nina. *Children's Games from Many Lands.* New York: Friendship Press, 1952.

Miller, Josephine V. *Paper Structure and Construction.* Peoria, Ill.: Bennett, 1957.

Miller, Mary. *Finger Play.* New York: Schirmer, n.d.

Moffitt, Mary. "Teaching Reading to Younger Children." *Pioneer Ideas in Education.* Washington, D.C.: U.S. Government Printing Office, 1962.

Moffitt, Mary W. *Learning Theory: Mathematics for Early Childhood, Educational Comments.* Toledo, Ohio: College of Education, University of Toledo, 1965.

Montessori, Maria. *Dr. Montessori's Own Handbook.* New York: Schocken Books, 1965.

————. *Spontaneous Activity in Education.* Cambridge, Mass.: Robert Bentley, Inc., 1917.

————. *Spontaneous Activity in Education.* New York: Schocken Books, 1965.

————. *The Montessori Elementary Material.* Cambridge, Mass.: Robert Bentley, Inc., 1964.

————. *The Montessori Method.* New York: Schocken Books, 1964.

Moore, Joan C., Margaret W. Palmer, and John E. Pate. *Handbook of Kindergarten Activities for Every Day of the Year.* Darien, Conn.: Teachers Publishing Corp., 1967.

Moustakas, Clark E., and Minnie P. Berson. *Young Children and Science.* Washington: Association for Childhood Education International, 1964.

Murphy, Lois. *Humanity.* Dimensions in Early Learning Series. San Rafael, Calif.: Dimensions Publishing Co., 1966.

————, et al. *The Widening World of Childhood.* New York: Basic Books, 1962.

Mussen, Paul H., et al. *Child Development and Personality.* New York: Harper and Row, 1969.

————, et al., eds. *Readings in Child Development and Personality.* New York: Harper & Row, 1969.

Nagel, Charles. *Skill Development through Games and Rhythmic Activities.* Palo Alto, Calif.: National Press, 1966.

National Advisory Council on the Education of Disadvantaged Children. *Report of the National Advisory Council on the Education of Disadvantaged Children.* Washington, D.C.: U.S. Government Printing Office, 1968.

National Association for Elementary School Principals. *National Elementary Principal.* September 1971, Early Childhood Education Issue.

National Association for the Education of Young Children. *Let's Play Outdoors.* New York, 1957.

————. *Space for Play: The Youngest Children.* New York, 1966.

————. *Water, Sand, and Mud as Play Materials.* New York, 1959.

Navarra, J. G. *The Development of Scientific Concepts in a Child.* New York: Teachers College, 1955.

Nelson, Mary J. *Music in Early Childhood.* Morristown, N.J.: Silver Burdett, 1952.

Nelson, R. C. "Children's Poetry Preferences." *Elementary English,* vol. 43, no. 3, pp. 247-251, 1966.

New Jersey State Department of Education. *Reading in the Kindergarten.* Trenton: New Jersey State Department of Education, 1964.

————. *Shall We Teach Formal Reading in the Kindergarten?* Trenton: New Jersey State Department of Education, 1964.

New York State Department of Education. *Equipment for Children in Kindergarten.* Albany: New York State Department of Education, 1960.

————. *Guides for Selection for Indoor and Outdoor Equipment and Materials.* Albany: New York State Department of Education, 1966.

Newman, M. S. *Mathematics Program on Pre-kindergarten, Kindergarten and Grade One.* New York: Society for the Experimental Study of Education, 1967.

O'Donnell, Patrick. *Motor and Haptic Learning.* Dimensions in Early Learning Series, San Rafael, Calif.: Dimensions Publishing Co., 1969.

Office of Economic Opportunity. *Equipment and Supplies.* Washington, D.C.: Office of Economic Opportunity, 1965.

Ontario Institute for Studies in Education. "Early Learning." *Interchange,* vol. 2, p. 2, 1971.

Pearl, Arthur, and Frank Reissman. *Nature Study and Science in the Nursery School.* Toronto, Canada: Department of Public Welfare, n.d.

Pendred, G. E. *Play Materials for Young Children.* New Rochelle, N.Y.: Melbourne University Press, American Branch, 1952.

Perryman, Lucile C. "Dramatic Play and Cognitive Development." *Journal of Nursery Education,* vol. 17, no. 4, pp. 184-185, 1962.

————. "Science and the Young Child." *Young Children,* October 1964, pp. 47-51.

Phi Delta Kappa, Inc. "Early Childhood Education." *Phi Delta Kappan,* March 1969. Special Issue.

Phillips, John L., Jr. *The Origins of Intellect: Piaget's Theory.* San Francisco: Freeman, 1969.

Piaget, Jean. *The Child's Conception of Numbers.* New York: Humanities Press, 1952.

————. *Language and Thought of the Child.* Trans. Marjorie Gabain. New York: Meridian Books, Inc., 1955.

————. *Play, Dreams and Imitation in Childhood.* Trans. Caleb Gattegno and P. M. Hodgson. New York: Norton, 1962.

————, and Barbel Inhelder. *The Psychology of the Child.* Trans. Helen Weaver. New York: Basic Books, 1969.

————, et al. *The Child's Concept of Geometry.* New York: Basic Books, 1960.

Picard, A. J. "Piaget's Theory of Development with Implication for Teaching Elementary School Mathematics." *School Science and Math,* vol. 69, pp. 275-280, 1969.

Pine, Tillie S., and Joseph Levine. *Water All Around.* New York: McGraw-Hill, 1959.

Pines, Maya. *Revolution in Learning: The Years from Birth to Six.* New York: Harper & Row, 1967.

Pitcher, Evelyn G., and Z. B. Ames. *The Guidance Nursery School.* New York: Harper & Row, 1964.

Pitcher, Evelyn G., et al. *Helping Young Children Learn.* Columbus, Ohio: Merrill, 1966.

Pluckrose, Henry. *Let's Work Large.* New York: Taplinger, 1967.

Pollack, Samuel, and Juliana Gensley. "When Do They Learn Geometry?" *Young Children,* vol. 20, no. 1, p. 52, 1964.

Portchmouth, John. *Creative Crafts for Today.* New York: Viking, 1970.

Portfolio for Kindergarten Teachers. Washington, D.C.: Association for Childhood Education International, 1951.

Prekindergarten Teacher's Guide. Dayton, Ohio: Dayton Public Schools, 1970-1971.

Project Head Start. *Daily Program 1.* Rainbow Series Book 4. Washington, D.C.: Office of Economic Opportunity, 1969.

———. *Daily Program 2.* Rainbow Series Book 7. Washington, D.C.: Office of Economic Opportunity, 1969.

———. *Daily Program 3.* Rainbow Series Book 11. Washington, D.C.: Office of Economic Opportunity, 1969.

———. *Primary Mathematics Magazine.* Washington, D.C.: Office of Economic Opportunity, 1969.

Rambusch, Nancy. *Learning How to Learn.* Baltimore: Helicon Press, 1962.

Read, Katharine. *The Nursery School: A Human Relations Lab.* Philadelphia: Saunders, 1966.

Reed, Carl, and Joseph Orze. *Art from Scrap.* Worcester, Mass.: Davis Publications, Inc., 1960.

Renfield, Richard. *If Teachers Were Free.* Washington, D.C.: Acropolis, 1969.

Riley, Carole. "Carpentry in the Nursery School." *Young Children,* October 1964.

Roanoke City Schools. *Kindergarten Resource Units: A Planning Aid for the Kindergarten Teacher.* Roanoke, Va.: Roanoke City Schools, 1968.

Robison, Helen, and Bernard Spodek. *New Directions in the Kindergarten.* New York: Teachers College, 1965.

Rosenberg, Martha. "Let Creative Music Unlock Their Imagination." *Journal of Nursery Education,* vol. 17, no. 3, pp. 126-127, 1962.

————. "Making Music Pictures with Rhythm Instruments." *Journal of Nursery Education,* vol. 18, no. 3, pp. 189-190, 1963.

Rowen, Betty. *Learning through Movement.* New York: Teachers College, 1963.

Rudolph, Marguerita, and Dorothy H. Cohen. "Many Purposes of Blockbuilding and Woodwork." *Young Children,* vol. 20, pp. 41-46, 1964.

Sava, Samuel G. "When Learning Comes Easy." *Saturday Review,* Nov. 16, 1968, pp. 102-104, 119.

Sawyer, Ruth. *The Way of a Storyteller.* New York: Viking, 1962.

————. *The Way of the Weather.* Basic Science Education Series. Evanston, Ill.: Row, Peterson, n.d.

Schaefer, Earl S. "Learning from Each Other." *Childhood Education,* October 1971, pp. 3-7.

Schoat, G. Warren, Jr. *Magic of Water.* New York: Scribner, 1955.

Schulman, Anne Shaaker. *Absorbed in Living.* Washington, D.C.: National Association for the Education of Young Children, 1967.

Scott, Louise B., and Jesse J. Thompson. *Rhymes for Fingers and Flannelboards.* New York: McGraw-Hill, 1960.

Sharp, Evelyn. *Thinking Is Child's Play.* New York: Dutton, 1969.

Shaw, Jean, and Maxine Schoggen. *Children Learning.* Nashville, Tenn.: George Peabody College for Teachers, 1969.

Sheehy, Emma D. *Children Discover Music and Dance.* New York: Teachers College, 1968.

Shipley, S. S. "Woodworking: Joy to Kindergarten Boys." *Instructor,* vol. 78, p. 45, 1969.

Shoemaker, Rowena. *All in Play.* New York: Play Schools Association, Inc., 1958.

————. "What Are Good Play Materials?" *Childhood Education,* March 1960, p. 14.

Smith R. B. "Effect of Group Vocal Training on the Singing Ability of Nursery School Children." *Journal of Research in Music Education,* vol. 11, no. 2, pp. 137-141, 1963.

Snyder, Alice. *Creating Music with Children.* New York: Mills Music Co., 1957.

Sponseller, Doris, ed. *Play as a Learning Medium.* Washington, D.C.: National Association for the Education of Young Children, 1974.

Stanley, Julian C., ed. *Preschool Programs for the Disadvantaged: Five Experimental Approaches to Early Childhood Education.* Proceedings, 1st Annual Hyman Blumberg Symposium on Research in Early Childhood Education. Baltimore, Md.: Johns Hopkins, 1972.

Starks, Ester B. *Blockbuilding.* Washington, D.C.: National Education Association, 1960.

———. "Dramatic Play." *Childhood Education,* vol. 37, no. 4, pp. 163-167, 1960.

Steere, Caryl, et al. *Indoor and Outdoor Spaces for 3 and 4 Year Olds.* Albany, N.Y.: State University of New York, n.d.

Stephens, Lois, and Wilbur H. Dutton. "Development of Time Concepts by Kindergarten Children." *School Science and Math,* vol. 69, no. 1, pp. 59-63, 1969.

Sterling, Dorothy. *Insects and the Homes They Build.* Garden City, N.Y.: Doubleday, 1961.

———, and Winifred Lubell. *Caterpillars.* Garden City, N. Y.: Doubleday, 1961.

Stevens, Dorothy. "A Sink with Running Water." *Journal of Nursery Education,* Spring 1959, p. 24.

Stevens, Harold. *Ways with Art: 50 Techniques for Teaching Children.* New York: Van Nostrand Reinhold, 1963.

Stiles, David R. *Fun Projects for Dad and Kids.* New York: Arco, 1963.

Strang, Ruth. *Reading.* Dimensions in Early Learning Series. San Rafael, Calif.: Dimensions Publishing Co., 1966.

Strobridge, Robert. *Aesthetics.* Dimensions in Early Learning Series. San Rafael, Calif.: Dimensions Publishing Co., 1966.

Swenson, Esther J. *Making Primary Arithmetic Meaningful to Children.* Washington, D.C.: National Education Association, 1961.

———. *Teaching Arithmetic to Children.* New York: Macmillan, 1964.

Teachers College, Columbia University. "The Family: First Instructor and Pervasive Guide." *Teachers College Record,* December 1974.

Teachers Publications. *Woodworking Projects for Elementary Grades.* Darien, Conn.: Teachers Publications, n.d.

Teel, D. A. "Creating with Wood." *Instructor,* vol. 78, pp. 54-55, 1968.

Thomas, Ronald, and Jane Moose. *Movement: The First Step to Learning.* Fayetteville, Ark.: Northwest Arkansas Supplementary Education Center, n.d.

Torrance, E. Paul. *Creativity.* Dimensions in Early Learning Series. San Rafael, Calif.: Dimensions Publishing Co., 1966.

————. *Rewarding Creative Behavior.* Englewood Cliffs, N. J.: Prentice-Hall, 1965.

Trager, H. S., and M. R. Yarno. *They Learn What They Live.* New York: Harper & Row, 1952.

Tritten, Gottfried. *Art Techniques for Children.* New York: Van Nostrand Reinhold, 1964.

Turner, E. M. *Teaching Aids for Elementary Mathematics.* New York: Holt, 1966.

Utley, Jean. *What's Its Name: A Guide to Speech and Hearing Development.* Urbana: University of Illinois Press, 1950.

Van der Eyken, Willem. *The Pre-school Years.* Baltimore: Penguin, 1967.

Van Hagen, Winifred, Genevive Dexter, and Jesse Williams. *Physical Education in the Elementary School.* Sacramento, Calif.: State Department of Education, 1951.

Victor, Edward. *Science for the Elementary School.* New York: Macmillan, 1965.

Vygotsky, L. S. *Thought and Language.* Cambridge, Mass.: M.I.T., 1962.

Wagner, Guy, et al. *Arithmetic Games for All Grades.* Darien, Conn.: Teachers Publishing Corp., 1964.

Wankelman, Willard, Philip Wigg, and Marietta Wigg. *A Handbook of Arts and Crafts.* Dubuque, Iowa: Wm. C. Brown, 1961.

Weaver, Kitty. *Lenin's Grandchildren: Preschool Education in the Soviet Union.* New York: Simon and Schuster, 1971.

Weber, Evelyn. *Early Childhood Education: Perspectives on Change.* Worthington, Ohio: Charles A. Jones Publishing Co., 1970.

Webster, Patricia Rowe. "How Much Structure in Nursery School?" *Offspring,* vol. 6, no. 2, pp. 4-9, 1965.

Weikart, David P., Constance Kamii, and Norma Radin. *Perry Preschool Project Progress Report.* Ypsilanti, Mich.: Ypsilanti Public Schools, 1964.

Westcott, Alvin M., and J. A. Smith. *Creative Teaching of Mathematics in the Elementary School.* Boston: Allyn and Bacon, 1967.

Western Publishing Co. *Whitman Creative Art Books.* (Constructing, Painting, Paper Art, Papier Mache, Print Art, Stitchery.) Racine, Wis., 1966.

Westman, Jack C., ed. *Individual Differences in Children.* New York: Wiley-Interscience, 1973.

Wetmore, Alexander, et al. *Water, Prey and Game Birds of North America.* Washington, D.C.: National Geographic Society, 1965.

White, Burton L. "Preschool: Has It Worked?" *Compact,* July-August 1973, pp. 6-7.

White, Robert W. "Motivation Reconsidered: The Concept of Competence." *Psychological Review,* vol. 66, pp. 297-333, 1959.

White, Sheldon. "Evidence for a Hierarchical Arrangement of Learning Processes." *Advances in Child Development and Behavior. Vol. 2.* Edited by L. R. Lipsitt and C. C. Spiker. New York: Academic, 1965.

Wilensky, Harold. *Observational Techniques in Preschool Classrooms.* New York: Bank Street College, n.d.

Winn, Marie, and Mary Ann Porcher. *The Playgroup Book.* Baltimore, Md: Penguin, 1969.

Winton, R. A., and Bernice Fleiss. "You're Asking Us: Of What Value Are Blockbuilding and Woodworking Activities?" *Instructor,* vol. 75, p. 29, 1966.

Wood, Nancy. *Verbal Learning.* Dimensions in Early Learning Series. San Rafael, Calif.: Dimensions Publishing Co., 1966.

Woodward, Virginia A. "Young Children Initiate Their Own Listening Experiences." *Young Children,* vol. 21, no. 1, pp. 9-12, 1965.

Wylie, Joanne, ed. *A Creative Guide for Preschool Teachers.* Racine, Wis.: Western Publishing Co., 1968.

Yamamoto, Kaoru, ed. *The Child and His Image: Self Concept in the Early Years.* Boston: Houghton Mifflin, 1972.

Young, Wesley A., and Gloria D. Miklowitz. *The Zoo Was My World.* New York: Dutton, 1969.

Zaffaroni, Joseph. "Patterns for Childhood Education in Science." *New Developments in Elementary School Science.* Washington, D.C.: National Science Teachers Association, National Education Association, 1963.

Zigler, Edward. "The Environmental Mystique: Training the Intellect versus Development of the Child." *Childhood Education,* May 1970, pp. 402–412.

———. "Myths and Facts: A Guide for Policymakers." *Compact,* July-August 1973, pp. 18-21.

Zigmond, Naomi, and Regina Cicci. *Auditory Learning.* Dimensions in Early Learning Series. San Rafael, Calif.: Dimensions Publishing Co., 1966.